INDOOR CRICKET

Avril Starling and Megan Lear

BLANDFORD PRESS
Poole · New York · Sydney

First published in the UK 1986 by Blandford Press,
Link House, West Street, Poole, Dorset BH15 1LL.

Copyright © 1986 Avril Starling & Megan Lear

British Library Cataloguing in Publication Data

Starling, Avril
  Indoor cricket.
  1. Indoor cricket.
  I. Title   II. Lear, Megan
  796.35'88   GV917

ISBN 0 7137 1906 0 (paperback)
      0 7137 1937 0 (hardback)

All rights reserved. No part of this book may
be reproduced or transmitted in any form or by
any means, electronic or mechanical, including
photocopying, recording or any information storage
and retrieval system, without permission in
writing from the Publisher.

Photography by Outlook Audio Visual Ltd
Typeset by Nene Phototypesetters Ltd, Northampton
Printed in Great Britain by
Bath Press, Avon

Contents

	Preface	7
1	The History of Indoor Cricket	9
2	The Rules of the Game	15
3	Techniques	37
4	Tactics	69
5	Training Practices for Indoor Cricket	77
	Index	95

This book is dedicated to
the loving memory of Avril's mother, Beryl Starling.

Preface

Indoor cricket is certainly a whole new ball game. It is a game for everyone, regardless of age or sex, and it has been enjoyed by people from all walks of life. Although it was started in Perth, Australia, initially as a means of training for the traditional game, this game is certainly not the same as traditional cricket. To the uninitiated, 'cricket' often means a staid game comprising involved skills and weird-sounding fielding positions. Indoor cricket transforms it into a fast, action-packed game that appeals to both traditionalists and non-cricketers alike.

It has been likened to a cross between cricket, indoor tennis and squash. For outdoor cricketers the benefits of this game are vast, but 80% of the people who play it are non-cricketers, and for them indoor cricket has been a whole new experience.

The purpose of this book is to outline the essence of the game and the skills and tactics that have developed in its short history. Many of the basic skills transfer directly from the traditional game and countless books have been written dealing with these in great detail; however, this book will concentrate on the specific skills and tactics that have developed as the game of indoor cricket has progressed.

(NB. Although one of the oustanding features of indoor cricket is the number of women who take part, for ease of reading we have followed the convention of referring to a player as 'he', 'him' etc.)

1
The History of Indoor Cricket

Indoor cricket is not only a sport but also a leisure activity. The success which the game has experienced in Australia and New Zealand is because it combines these two aspects like no other game. One reason is that indoor cricket is a commercially run game.

Apart from being a new sport which is accessible to most people, indoor cricket certainly owes its popularity to the traditional game.

There have indeed been many versions of cricket played indoors, which have preceded this game; some of these were used as a means of coaching, others as a way of playing cricket in the winter months when it is not possible to play outside. Two such games are continuous cricket and six-a-side cricket. The latter has very firm roots in England: national championships are held every year, the finals being played at the Lords' Indoor Cricket School. Six-a-side cricket is a modified version of the traditional game for which a hard ball is used and pads and protective gear are worn.

Traditional cricket enjoyed an increase in following and popularity with the advent of the one-day, limited-over match in the 1960s. Further developed in the late 1970s by Australian entrepreneur Kerry Packer, one-day, limited-over cricket, with its fast action and noisy crowds, was brought into the homes of sports fans in Australia via television coverage. This renewed interest in cricket convinced Paul Hanna, a property developer, that team cricket could be played indoors at a competitive level and that it would eventually become a major leisure pastime. In partnership with a friend, Mick Jones, he worked on the idea of a cricket game which, by eliminating the risk factors of traditional cricket such as the use of the hard ball, would appeal to a vast number of people.

At that stage neither Hanna nor Jones had much money

An ICA stadium in Australia.

between them but they managed to raise a $20,000 loan to convert a factory unit that they leased in the Morley Industrial Estate, Perth, Western Australia into their first two-court indoor cricket centre which was opened in August 1979.

The objectives of this new game, in which the use of a tennis ball encased in leather meant that no protective gear was necessary, were entertainment and enjoyment, a game that anyone could play. By surrounding the pitches with nets the game became much faster than traditional cricket; this inevitably increased the potential appeal of the game. All this is borne out by the fact that in Australia in 1986 one million people were playing each week, of which 25% were women.

It took about 18 months to develop the game and to straighten out the concepts and the rules. In January 1981 another centre was opened in Balcatta, Perth. In March 1981, Indoor Cricket Arenas (ICA) opened a four-court arena in Lurnea, Sydney, New South Wales. The expansion of the game under the ICA banner continued with ICA opening in Victoria in April 1981, and in Queensland in January 1982. September 1982 saw the opening of an ICA arena in Australian Capital Territory. By August 1983, ICA had opened in Tasmania with the South Australian opening occurring two months later. By 1986, Australia boasted over 300 stadia; ICA operated approximately 90 of these, and most of the rest were independent.

New Zealand's first indoor cricket stadium opened in Christchurch at the end of 1982, with a second opening a couple of months later at Whangerei. The first centre in Auckland was

The fact that indoor cricket caters just as much for women as for men is one of its greatest strengths. (Photo by courtesy of Cannon Ball Cricket)

opened in January 1983 at Mount Eden. In 1986 there were over 30 indoor cricket stadia in New Zealand, seven of which belonged to the ICA chain, the rest being independents.

England's first stadium specifically designed for a type of indoor cricket was opened in 1984 in Nottingham. 1985 saw Indoor Cricket Stadiums (ICS) opening stadia in Peterborough, Ipswich and Wellingborough. Other centres opened in 1985 included Redball in Sheffield and Cannon Ball (CBC) in Hounslow.

Indoor cricket is also played in South Africa and Papua New Guinea.

Since the early days, the stadia have become very sophisticated leisure/sporting complexes. ICA, probably the largest single operator in Australia, has arenas throughout the country. Its flagship is the Subiaco complex in Perth, which was converted from an existing warehouse and is regarded as the Lord's of indoor cricket. The complex includes a swimming pool, a gymnasium, squash and a restaurant as well as the indoor cricket courts. Most indoor cricket stadia in England have bar and snack bar or restaurant facilities to create the social atmosphere that is so much a part of the game.

That indoor cricket does have its roots in cricket was shown in November 1985, when part of the Lord's Indoor Cricket School was converted to accommodate two indoor courts.

As the game developed, so did the equipment used. Although stadia provide the equipment necessary, some players in Australia and New Zealand who are now taking the sport

David Gower takes guard, Paul Downton behind the stumps. (Photo by courtesy of Cannon Ball Cricket)

This time Gower and Downton are batting together. Downton is going to be lucky not to be run out! (Photo by courtesy of Cannon Ball Cricket)

Typical indoor cricket equipment.

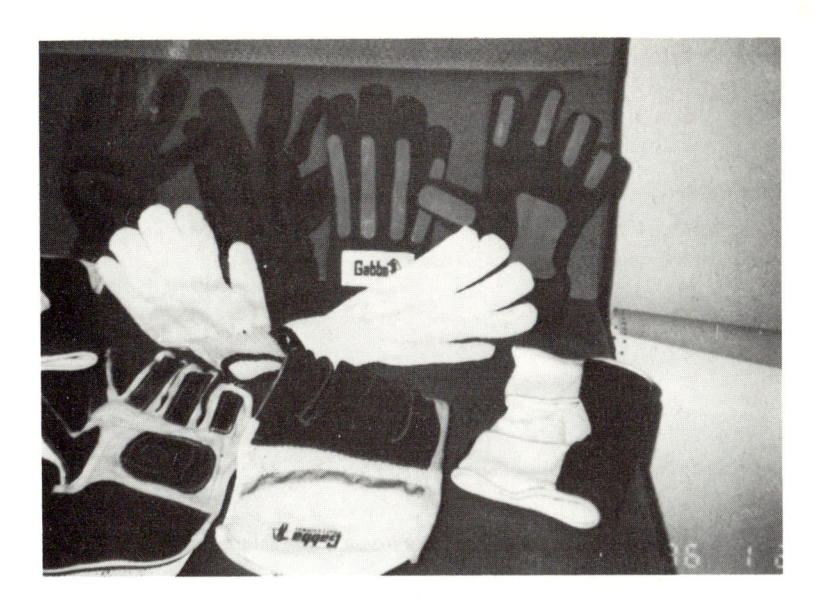

very seriously, and who are perhaps aiming for State and International honours, are using their own bats. Indoor bats are much lighter than the traditional bat, but because of the constant impact with the often concrete floor they have to be very strong. For this reason some are manufactured with a fibreglass toe.

There have also been developments with safety straps attached to the bats. The main reason batters wear gloves is to absorb perspiration as slippery hands could be dangerous when swinging a bat in a small space. At the Grafton Stadium in New South Wales head injuries were caused by flying bats, and this was the first stadium to introduce a simple safety strap attached to the bat to solve the problem. Some players playing at a high level have also started wearing eye-protectors similar to those used by squash players.

Playing clothing has also developed to a great extent. Certainly in ICA, ICS, Cannon Ball and Redball stadia, players are penalised for wearing non-conforming uniform. In Australia this playing gear has become very sophisticated. Some Australian centres offer a 'rent-a-shirt' service where players arriving without the correct team shirt may rent a shirt from the arena so that they conform with the matching shirt regulations.

Indoor cricket involves a lot of diving as players try to stop bonus runs being scored. For this reason many top league players wear protective knee and elbow-pads similar to those worn for volleyball; these were introduced by ICA in 1985. Specialised trousers with velcro knee-pads have also been devised so that the area most worn out by constant diving can easily be replaced.

Indoor cricket is played in most stadia in graded leagues. In Australia and New Zealand where the game has been longer established, other competitions involve teams from several stadia. In Auckland, for example, the ICA Premier League consists of the top ten teams in Auckland while the Superleague is similar to a provincial league in that it includes ICA teams from Whangerei, Auckland and Hamilton.

Players in Australia compete for State honours and 1982 saw the first ICA Australasian Championships. In 1985 these were held at the Tullamarine arena, Melbourne, Victoria. Each state team is selected from players competing in ICA competitions. The competition at these championships is very serious, with State sides practising together under the direction of coaches for several months beforehand.

Both in Australia and New Zealand there are Indoor Cricket Federations. In Australia the Indoor Cricket Federation organises its own version of national championships. In New Zealand the Federation has divided the country into regions and has organised regional and national championships.

Current international cricket stars have been attracted to play in exhibition games. To date no team of international outdoor Test stars has beaten an ICA indoor representative side, not even Clive Lloyd's West Indies team, who played the Western Australian State side in a shopping centre in Perth.

The highest accolade that any sportsperson can achieve is to represent their country at their chosen sport. Indoor cricket achieved the goal of international competition in July 1985, when teams of top players were selected from the national championships to represent New Zealand and Australia in a Test series.

Indoor cricket has come a long way since its beginnings in Perth in 1979. As it has progressed, more and more players have been drawn to this fast, action-packed sport. Not only is it a great participation sport but it is also very colourful and exciting for the spectator: in September 1984 the Australian ICA Superleague series was televised for the first time. The players themselves, regardless of age or ability, want to gain a greater understanding of the game and its tactics, and the purpose of the next chapters is to help all of them to gain the most enjoyment from this addictive sport.

2
The Rules of the Game

Two of the reasons why indoor cricket is a game that appeals to everyone are because the rules are simple and because they have been adapted to accommodate the growing number of women who are playing the game: they are devised to give a fast, action-packed game that anyone can play at any level.

The game is played between two teams consisting of a maximum of eight players; teams can of course be mixed. The game is played on a floodlit court surrounded by rebound netting on all four sides and with a netting roof. The court measures 28 metres long by 11 metres wide. The length of the wicket is the same as in the traditional game: 22 yards.

So it's cricket, but it *is* different. You don't wear pads and the ball is softer: originally a tennis ball in a plastic casing surrounded by leather. Each member of the team bats for four overs with a partner and everyone has to bowl two eight-ball

An empty court, showing lines and markings and scoring zones.

overs. The game consists of two innings, one per team, each of 16 overs. All these are bowled from the same end with the batters changing ends at the end of each over.

A feature of the game that guarantees involvement for everyone concerned is that when you're out, you're not out! You simply lose five runs from your team's score and you stay there until you and your partner have faced your four eight-ball overs. All this is shown on the electronic scoreboard, which is operated by the umpire; he sits high above the game and gives a ball-by-ball update on proceedings.

Scoring runs in this game is somewhat similar to the traditional indoor six-a-side game played so extensively in England, in that when the ball is hit into zones in the rebound netting, bonus runs are scored. Runs may also be scored by the batters running between the wickets. Here again, this game differs from the traditional game of cricket in that the non-striking batter stands halfway down the wicket, so that the distance to be run is much shorter.

An added feature is that the batter may be caught out after the ball has been hit into the netting; this does not include the six net in open competition, but in mixed competition a batter may be caught out off the six net. Once again this tends to make the game very fast, the angles at which the ball rebounds from the netting being similar to those in squash.

Perhaps what makes the game so very fast and active for the participants and exciting for the spectators is that the ball is never 'dead'. In the traditional game, when the ball comes to rest in the wicketkeeper's gloves or when the umpire is satisfied that the ball has come to rest with a fielder and that it is being relayed gently back to the bowler and the batters do not intend to take any further runs, the ball is deemed to be 'dead'. The ball is also 'dead' when a boundary is scored. None of this applies to indoor cricket. In indoor cricket the ball is always 'live' except when a wicket falls or the umpire calls 'time out' or 'over', and in the rare events of the ball leaving the playing area, coming into contact with a fielder before reaching the batting crease, or becoming entangled in any boundary equipment. This means that the batters have every opportunity to sneak runs – and, as they become more expert, they do! Batters in indoor cricket may sneak runs whilst the ball is being relayed back to the bowler, and even whilst the bowler is turning to walk back to his mark.

Batters bait the fielding side by moving from their respective creases, hoping the fielders will take the bait, throw the ball and

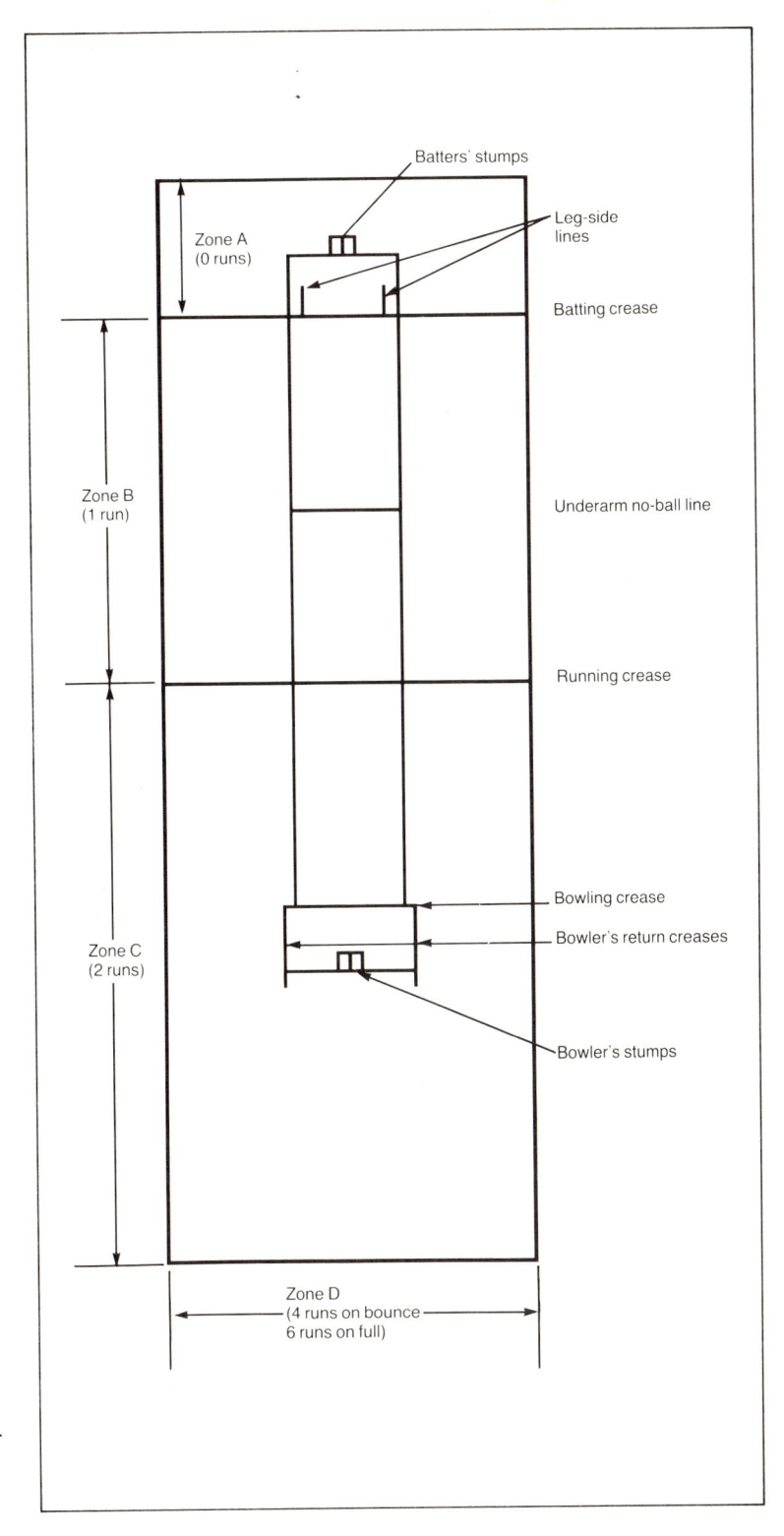

An indoor cricket court. The running crease is where the non-striker stands. For an explanation of the underarm no-ball line see page 26, and of the leg-side lines see page 24.

thus enable the batters to complete a further run. All this is in total contrast to the traditional game and as teams become more conversant with the rules these tactics soon develop. They will be dealt with in more detail in the chapter specifically concerned with tactics.

There are basic field-placings which have to be adhered to according with the rules. These state that there shall be no more than four players of the fielding team either side of the running crease at the moment that the ball is bowled. As in any game, the actual positions vary within this basic rule, according to the state of the game and the tactics being used. These will be dealt with in depth in the chapter on tactics.

FIELDING A TEAM

The two sides of eight players each may be open (male and/or female) teams or mixed teams – see page 32. One of these players will be the nominated captain. As in all team games the captain must nominate the team before the toss for innings and once the team has been nominated it may not be changed. If a team arrives with only six players they forfeit the toss at the discretion of the opposing captain.

Having said that, a team is allowed to play without the full complement of eight players, but there are certain penalties. ICS in England state that if a team short of players is batting and is still short after 12 overs of their innings, the fielding captain has the right to nominate the one or two players to bat again, depending on the number of players short. CBC, ICA in

A basic field-placing with four players in each half.

Australia and Redball in Sheffield state that if there is one player short from the batting side at the completion of the twelfth over, the captain of the bowling side chooses two batters who may not bat again. In this instance in the ICA rules the seventh batter will then bat the last four overs with each of the four unexcluded batters, who will bat one over each, or with one player who bats for the four overs. Both captains must be in agreement as to the choice of the batter. Furthermore, in accordance with these rules the seventh batter must face the first ball of each of the last four overs. Redball's ruling is that the seventh batter bats the last four remaining overs with one of the four other batters.

Under both ICA and Redball rules, the batting side will incur a five-run penalty for any player who is missing from the batting innings and if a player is missing for the whole game, his team will incur a ten-run batting penalty which will be deducted from their batting score.

ICA and Redball rules state that if there are *two* players short from the batting side, the captain of the bowling side again chooses two batters who may not bat again. The remaining four unexcluded batters then bat in pairs for two overs per pair. The batting side also incurs a ten-run penalty which is deducted at the start of the thirteenth over. ICA also state that if the two players remain absent for the whole game, a 20-run penalty is deducted from the team's batting score.

Under the ICS rules, five runs are deducted for each player missing at the start of the game, but the penalty remains at five runs even if the player is missing for the whole of the game. Also in the ICS rules the proviso is made for a fielding team short of players. Here the captain of the batting side will choose two (or four if the fielding side is two short) to bowl the extra overs. This means that if by the twelfth over of the game the fielding team is still one player short, two players from that fielding team will be nominated by the captain of the batting team to bowl one extra over each. This has to be stated at the end of the twelfth over so that the players who have to bowl again do so in the last four overs of the game. All members of the fielding side must by then have bowled at least one over.

CBC, ICA and Redball have similar rulings on the absence of players from the bowling side. If one player is missing, a five-run penalty is automatically deducted from their batting innings. The extra two overs must be bowled by two different bowlers and they must be the last two of the innings. The opposing captain elects two players who may not bowl again, the last two overs being bowled by any two of the five unexcluded players. Similarly, if there are two players short from the bowling side, they immediately incur a ten-run penalty deducted from their batting innings. The overs of the two absent players must be the last four of the innings; the captain of the batting side chooses two players who may not bowl again, and the four other bowlers bowl one over each.

It is not essential for the fielding team to have a wicketkeeper in the traditional sense of the word. Different companies have different rules about the position of the wicketkeeper, although they all agree that the wearing of wicketkeeping gloves is optional. ICS and CBC state that a fielder is considered to be the wicketkeeper only if he stands behind the stumps and in line with the pitch. If a fielder wearing gloves stands anywhere else, the umpire will call a no-ball. However, under the ICA rules, the wicketkeeper, wearing gloves, may stand anywhere in Zone A.

SUBSTITUTES

Players may be substituted only in the case of illness or injury which has occurred during the course of the game. The opposing captain has the right to object if the substitute is not of similar ability to the player who has become incapacitated. Substitutes are not permitted to bowl. If, however, the injured player becomes fit to rejoin the game he may do so, despite the fact that he has had a substitute fielding for him.

If a team becomes short of a batter or bowler through injury, a player may be nominated to bat or bowl the injured player's current over at the time of the injury. In this instance it does not matter whether the nominated player has already batted or bowled. If, however, the injury occurs in the bowler's first over, the second over must be taken after the twelfth over and another player may be nominated to bowl this by the opposing captain.

As in traditional cricket, a runner may be allowed for a batter who has become injured during the course of the game. This may only occur with the approval of the umpire. The ICA code of rules states that the opposing captain has the right to choose who the runner will be. Again, as in traditional cricket, the runner must wear gloves and carry a bat. The injured batter, when not facing, must stand in Zone A. As in traditional cricket, the injured batter may be stumped or run out should either he or his runner be out of their ground.

EQUIPMENT

All the equipment necessary for indoor cricket is provided by the stadium, including bats, balls and gloves. Players are allowed to provide their own bats and gloves but they may only be used at the discretion of the umpire. The rules applying to the wearing of batting gloves vary slightly according to the stadium being played in. Having said that, all stadia insist on the wearing of at least one batting glove and some insist, as ICS do, that two batting gloves must be worn. Wicketkeeping gloves are also provided by the stadium and again the wearing of these is optional. Wicketkeepers are also allowed to wear the cotton batting gloves provided by the stadium.

SCORING

As already indicated (see page 16), bonus runs are scored by hitting the netting in the different zones, according to which zone's net the ball strikes first. When a striker hits the ball into the Zone D netting either four or six runs may be scored. Four runs will be scored if the ball strikes the Zone D net having first touched the floor and six runs will be scored if the ball hits the Zone D netting on the full. The roof netting is only a restrictive boundary net and bonus runs are not given for hitting it. If the ball hits the roof netting and then passes to the Zone D net on the full, six runs will be scored.

ICA, ICS and CBC give one bonus run only for the zone from the batting crease to the runner's crease (Zone B) whilst Redball also give one bonus run for the area behind the batting crease (Zone A).

When the batters cross, one from the running crease to the batting crease and the other vice versa after hitting the ball or at any time when the ball is in play, one run is scored. This may be done at any time except when the ball is dead, and is in addition to any bonus runs scored against the netting. No run is scored if a batter is run out while trying to complete it.

If any member of the fielding side misfields or deflects the ball into the net after the ball has been hit by the striker the bonus runs for that zone will apply. Overthrows into the netting do not apply however, so if the fielder throws, flicks or kicks the ball into the netting whilst attempting to run out a batter, no runs are added. The ICA and CBC rules do indicate that the umpire may use his discretion as to whether the ball is under control, and if in his opinion it is not, the bonus runs will be scored.

If the ball when bowled hits the striking batter's body, regardless of whether a shot has been played, and rebounds into the netting zones, no bonus runs will be awarded. The batters may, however, cross for a run. However, if the ball, having been hit by the striker into the non-striking batter's body, rebounds into the netting, the bonus runs for that zone are awarded.

THE UMPIRE

The umpire is responsible for all the decisions in the game. He sits in the umpire's stand high above the play behind the striking batter. Regardless of the stadium in which he sits, his job is always the same: the umpire is the sole judge of fair and unfair play and in all disputes, the umpire's decision is final. Unlike traditional cricket where there are two umpires in charge of the game, in indoor cricket one umpire is solely in charge of the proceedings. Once again, indoor cricket differs from the traditional game in that the umpire, not a separate scorer, is responsible for the scoring of the game.

The indoor cricket umpire scores in two ways. The first way is by operating the console which controls the electronic scoreboard. He also records the results of each delivery on a scoresheet and gives a ball-by-ball account of the play over a microphone as he calls every decision made and every run scored. His job is very involved and the training of the umpires is vital.

Scoreboards vary from company to company but the basis of them is the same. During the first innings only the top right-hand box and bottom left-hand box are in operation. The top right-hand box shows the number of the over that the fielding side is bowling; the bottom left-hand box indicates the current score.

When the first batting side have completed their allotted 16 overs their final total score is transferred to the top left-hand box.

The second batting side's current score now appears in the bottom left-hand box. The bottom right-hand box shows the comparative score of the first batting team at the start of the over indicated in the top right-hand box. So during the second batting team's innings all four boxes are in operation.

In some stadia, as with the equipment at the Lord's Indoor Cricket School, the scoreboard gives a ball-by-ball account of the game as the scoresheet has a computer printout which

An indoor cricket scoreboard during the second innings of a match. The top right-hand box sometimes shows which ball is being bowled in the over, as well. The bottom right-hand box sometimes shows the runs needed per ball during the rest of the innings to overtake the total of the side batting first.

Score of side batting first → 150

Number of overs elapsed at completion of current over ← 14

Current score of batting side → 132

Score at the start of the equivalent over in the first innings ← 129

involves the umpire in less work. However, the basic principle behind the scoreboard is the same and the job of the umpire the same, regardless of stadium.

The umpire is totally responsible for the conduct of the game and may from time to time call 'time out' for various reasons or at the request of the batting or fielding sides. However, the umpire does have the right to refuse to allow 'time out' if it is called too often. It is the umpire's decision whether the ball is in play or dead. As soon as the umpire is satisfied that all players have taken up their positions, he calls 'play' and from that moment on the ball is in play, that is 'live'. As part of the distinction between the ball being in play or dead, the umpire must decide whether a batter has faced up in his stance before the ball is bowled. The other instances of 'dead ball' were dealt with earlier (page 16).

The umpire, being responsible for the conduct of the game, is also responsible for decisions on dismissals, which will be dealt with in more detail later in this chapter. The umpire shall not, however, give a batter out unless appealed to by the opposing side. This appeal must be prior to the next ball or, in the case of the last ball of the over, before 'over' is called. An appeal covers all forms of dismissal and it must be made in the form of a verbal question to the umpire. In all cases, the umpire's decision is final, though he is at liberty to alter his decision provided that this is done promptly.

The umpire is responsible for calling 'over' and in indoor cricket this often becomes a vital call. The rules state that 'over' shall be called when the correct number of balls have been delivered and the ball is held securely at either the wicket-keeper's or the bowler's stumps. Often this does not happen and in order to call 'over', the umpire must be certain that both teams have ceased to think that the ball is live and in play; in other words, the batting side is not endeavouring to sneak runs and the fielding side is not baiting batters with 'dummy' throws.

WIDES

Wides and no-balls transfer from the traditional game of cricket and also apply in indoor cricket, the former being very strictly umpired.

Off-side wides are called if the ball passes on the striking batter's off-side outside the intersection of the batting crease and the edge of the pitch without being touched by the striking batter's equipment or body.

Leg-side wides are more strictly umpired in that the distance is not as lenient. In all stadia there are leg-side lines drawn on the batting crease; a leg-side wide will be called if the ball lands on the pitch on the batter's leg-side, outside the intersection of the leg-side line with the batting crease. The distance of this line from the middle stump varies. In ICA arenas in Australia the distance is 30 cms whilst in ICS stadia in England it is 50 cms and in CBC 45 cms. ICA and CBC also call it a wide when the ball passes over the striking batter's shoulder, regardless of whether it does so on the full or after bouncing, when the batter is in his normal batting stance. However, in some stadia in England this has been changed and now becomes defined as a no-ball.

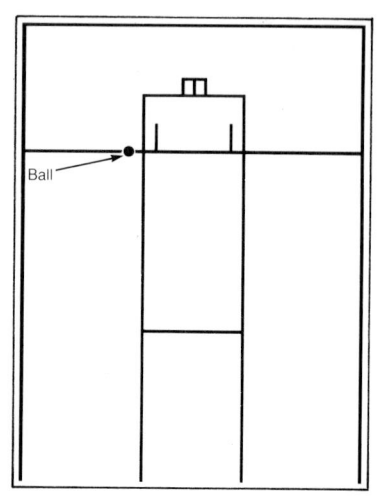

The ball is passing outside the intersection of the batting crease.

The ball is passing outside the mark for the leg-side wide; this incurs a two-run penalty.

The front foot is completely clear of the bowling crease and therefore this is a no-ball.

The front foot is on the bowling crease; this is not a no-ball.

Wides count as part of the over and no extra delivery is received by the batter, except as detailed in the next paragraph. A penalty of two runs is added to the batting team's score for each wide bowled. A batter may only be dismissed off a wide by being run out, stumped or by interference.

The ICS and CBC rules have further penalised a bowler who bowls a wide in the last over of the innings. The game of indoor cricket is decided upon runs scored during an innings of 16 overs. It therefore becomes very easy for a bowler to bowl negatively in the last over, bowl three wides and give away six runs when the bowler is aware that the batting side require, say, 13 runs to win. To counteract this negative approach, if a wide is bowled during the last over of an innings the umpire will award the penalty runs and require the ball to be bowled again.

NO-BALLS

As with wides, a no-ball incurs a two-run penalty and no extra ball is delivered, with the exception of a no-ball being bowled in the last over of an innings in ICS or CBC stadia where the penalty runs are awarded and the ball bowled again.

Once again, it is the umpire's decision on a no-ball which is final. The umpire will call a no-ball if at the point of delivery the front foot is in front of and clear of the bowling crease and/or either foot is clearly outside the bowler's return crease. The ball will also be called a no-ball if it hits the roof netting before pitching, if more than four members of the fielding side are in either half of the playing area or if a fielder other than the bowler moves onto the pitch before the ball is bowled.

A bowler will furthermore be penalised the statutory two runs if the ball lands off the pitch on the full. A no-ball will also be called if the umpire considers that the ball has been thrown and not bowled.

Because the people who play indoor cricket range from the total non-sportsman right through to the county, State, province or perhaps international cricketer, there are rules specially devised for the player who bowls underarm. The underarm

No-balls.

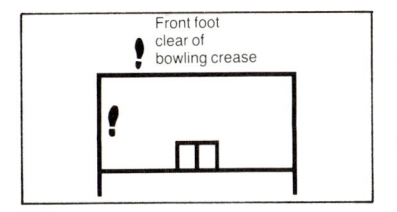

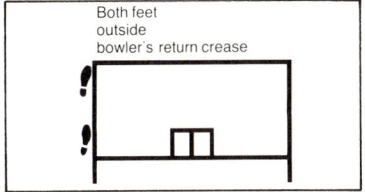

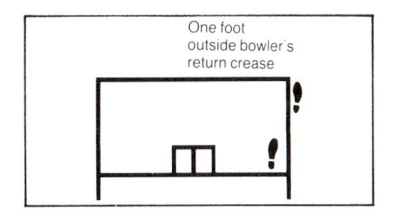

Five fielders are in the front half of the court before the ball has been released by the bowler; this is a no-ball.

The fielder is clearly standing on the pitch before the ball is bowled; this is a no-ball.

line is clearly marked on the diagram on page 17. If the ball, having been bowled underarm, fails to pitch over this line, the ball will be called a no-ball and the usual two-run penalty incurred.

A player is totally at liberty to bowl underarm but if that player changes his style to overarm during the course of an over without informing the umpire, a no-ball will be called. Likewise, if a bowler changes sides of the wicket from over to round or vice versa during the course of an over without informing the umpire a no-ball will be called.

A batter may be dismissed off a no-ball only by being run out or by interference. Batters may also score from a no-ball in any of the ways already described. However, regardless of whether the ball is hit into a netted zone or not, or whether the batters cross or not, they will be awarded a minimum of two runs plus any runs taken. The diagram below shows the runs awarded for hitting a no-ball into a netted zone and the batters also crossing for a run.

In ICA arenas in Australia a striking batter is permitted to hit a delivery only after it has passed over the underarm line. If the ball fails to do this the umpire calls 'dead ball', but the delivery counts as part of the over and incurs a minimum of a two-run penalty.

DISMISSALS

All dismissals automatically cause the batting team to lose five runs from their team's score. A batter may be out in one of many ways, some of which transfer directly or in an adapted form from traditional cricket and some of which are specific to indoor cricket.

Bowled

A batter may be out bowled if the striking batter's wicket is bowled down and the bails are dislodged, regardless of whether the ball first touched the striking batter's body or equipment.

It is worth noting at this stage that the wicket is deemed to be down when either the ball or the striking batter's bat or person completely removes either bail from the stumps; however, a disturbance of a bail does not constitute a complete removal. The wicket is also deemed to be down if any player completely removes a bail from the top of the stumps with his hand, provided of course that the hand is holding the ball. It is important that before being struck the stumps must be upright. The stumps, as long as they are standing, are always live, regardless of whether the bails have been removed during play. If the bails have been removed during the course of play, the stumps may be hit again and the batter may be given out.

Caught

A batter may be given out caught if the ball, having been hit by the striking batter's bat or hand holding the bat, is caught before it touches the ground. The striking batter will also be given out if the ball having been hit then hits the striker's body or vice versa before being caught.

A catch may also be taken off all boundary netting except a direct hit to the six net. However, if the ball hits the side netting in either Zone B or C, passes onto the six net and is then caught, the striker will be given out. Conversely, should the ball pass

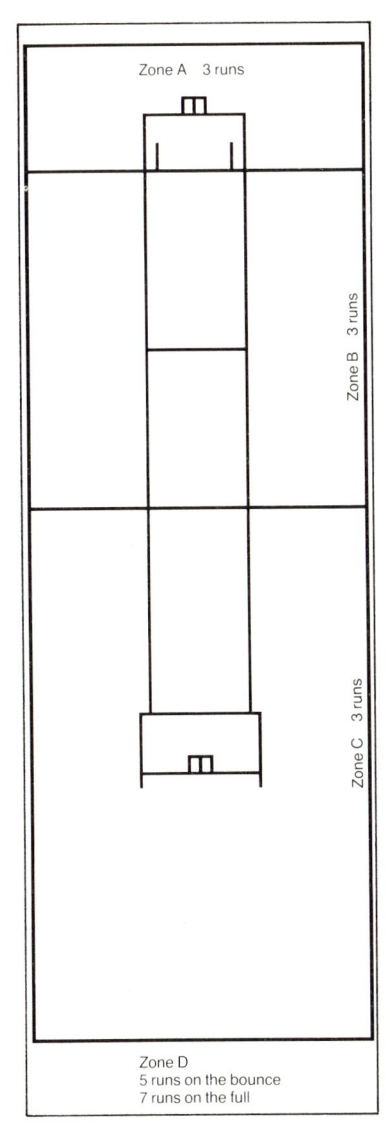

Zone A 3 runs
Zone B 3 runs
Zone C 3 runs
Zone D
5 runs on the bounce
7 runs on the full

The total runs that are scored if a no-ball is hit into a scoring zone and the batters cross once.

through a fielder's hands directly onto the back net and then be caught, the striking batter is not out. This rule, however, differs in mixed competition, and this will be dealt with later.

Finally, the striking batter is out caught if the ball is hit directly into the non-striking batter and then caught.

Hit wicket
A means of dismissal which is akin to traditional cricket is being out by hitting one's own wicket. This really is exactly as the name describes in that the striking batter will be given out if he breaks his own wicket, that is dislodges the bails, whilst attempting to play the ball or whilst setting off for the first run immediately after playing at the ball. A batter will not be given out in this manner if he breaks the wicket whilst making his ground, that is in striving to 'get in'.

The batter has moved back too close to his stumps and has hit his own wickets.

LBW
The lbw means of dismissal, often so controversial in the traditional outdoor game, is very much simplified in this game. With the umpire sitting high above the play and behind the striking batter, it has to be simple to give the umpire the best possible opportunity of adjudging it. A striking batter can only be out lbw if the ball strikes his body and he has made no

The batter is in front of the stumps when the ball hits his leg and has offered no shot; this is out, LBW.

The batter is in a similar position but has offered a shot and therefore cannot be given out.

The batter is moving across and deliberately interfering with the fielder who is attempting to field the ball; this is out, interference.

attempt to hit the ball, so if any shot is offered this means of dismissal does not apply. As with all means of dismissal, the fielding side must appeal and in order for the umpire to give the striking batter out he must be assured that the ball would have hit the stumps, regardless of where the ball has pitched.

Interference

A batter may be dismissed in indoor cricket for interference; this is equivalent to being adjudged out for obstruction in the traditional game of cricket. There are basically three ways in which this may occur. The first is when either the striker or non-striking batter deliberately interferes with the ball whilst it is in play, whether he deliberately kicks it out of the way whilst attempting a run, or handles the ball. Once again the fielding side must appeal and as with any appeal, the final decision rests with the umpire. The second sort of interference is when a striker or a non-striking batter deliberately obstructs a member of the fielding team, as the fielder has the right of way if he is attempting to field the ball. Thirdly, as in the traditional game, the striking batter is permitted to take steps in order to prevent the ball from striking his wicket, but he may not deliberately strike or stop the ball more than once; if he does he may, on appeal, be adjudged out.

Run out

It is worth mentioning at this stage that a batter is considered to be out of his ground unless some part of the bat in hand or the body is grounded behind the line of the batting crease or the running crease. The important part to note here is that it must be grounded behind the line as on the line is deemed as out.

The principles involved in being run out are similar to those in traditional cricket, with the obvious exception that the non-striking batter stands halfway down the pitch on the running crease. A batter is adjudged to be run out if in running he is out of his ground and a member of the fielding team breaks the wicket. It must be remembered that a batter is run out at the non-striking end by the wicket being broken at the bowler's stumps.

The question of breaking the wickets is important here. It has already been stated that the stumps do not need to be remade with the bails in position, but they must be upright in order for an appeal to be valid. This is very often of importance in this fast game where batters are always looking out for extra runs.

The fielder has made a direct hit on the stumps at the bowler's end before the batter has made his ground at the running crease. Out, run out.

The wicketkeeper has removed the bails with the ball in his gloves and the batter's foot is clearly out of her ground. Out, stumped.

Stumped

With the batters always endeavouring to score extra runs and with the wicketkeeper often standing up behind the stumps, stumpings are frequent in indoor cricket. The striking batter can be out stumped if in missing the ball he is out of his ground and the wicketkeeper breaks the wickets with the ball or with the hand holding the ball. The wicketkeeper in indoor cricket, unlike in the traditional game, may take the ball in front of the stumps, but in order to stump a batter the wicketkeeper must remove the bails from either the side or behind the stumps. If the ball hits the wicketkeeper and rebounds from his body onto the wickets and the bails are thus removed, the batter on appeal will be given out if he is out of his ground. But if the ball hits the netting and rebounds onto the stumps without having first touched the wicketkeeper, the batter is not out.

'Mankad'

Perhaps the most controversial of all indoor cricket rules is that referring to 'mankad'. This means of dismissal refers to the non-striking batter leaving his running crease before the ball

The bowler has removed the bail as the backing-up batter is out of his ground. Out, mankad.

has been delivered. The bowler, without warning that batter, is allowed to break the wickets with the hand holding the ball and the non-striking batter on appeal may be given out 'mankad' if he is out of his ground. This does not count as part of the over.

As tactics and games have become more intense and competitive, batters are constantly trying to sneak a few extra inches in order to gain their ground. In essence, leaving the running crease before the ball is delivered is tantamount to cheating and so this rule is very firmly adhered to. By the same token, however, bowlers are constantly on the look-out for a mankad and try to deceive the non-striking batter into thinking the ball is to be released and so leaving the running crease. ICS and CBC have tried to stop this by a rule which states that any undue time-wasting may incur a penalty, the severity of which is at the discretion of the umpire. This has been implemented to try to stop bowlers trying for a mankad when the non-striking batter is clearly still in his ground.

Many traditional cricketers who play the indoor game have found it hard to come to terms with this rule, as in outdoor cricket the etiquette is to give the non-striking batter a warning. However, in indoor cricket it is very necessary to stop the batter sneaking those extra yards – remember, it amounts to cheating!

MIXED RULES

All the rules outlined so far refer to open competition. Females are permitted to play in male sides but no allowance is made for them. It is not the case in reverse: males are not allowed to play in female competition! There are, however, certain rules which apply specifically to mixed competition, and these should be read in conjunction with the main rules already detailed.

The rules state that a mixed team may not contain more than four males; it may, however, contain more females so that the split may be five females and three males or six females and two males.

When batting the pairs should be mixed, and when fielding the order of bowling must alternate.

If players are absent from a mixed team and if the team is short of female players, the remaining females must be the players to bowl and bat again. This means that if a mixed team is two females short, the remaining two females must bowl the last four overs and bat for four overs each with a male partner. CBC, ICA and Redball state that if the mixed team is only one female short, any two of the remaining females must bowl the last two overs; this must of course be approved of by the opposing captain. All the females must bat and one will have to bat twice, with the fourth male during the last four overs of the innings. The normal penalties as described earlier will be applied. ICS state that if a mixed team is one female short, one of the remaining females must bowl the last two overs, her selection

There are two males and two females fielding in the front half of the court.

once again subject to the approval of the opposition captain. The rules about batting are the same as those implemented by ICA, Redball and CBC.

Substitution in mixed competition is quite straightforward in that if a player needs to be substituted during the course of the game, the substitute player must be of the same sex. Similarly, a runner for an injured batter must be of the same sex.

The rules for the mixed game are weighted so that a female may not be taken advantage of and so that the males may not simply use brute strength. This is apparent when looking at the means of scoring in mixed competition. A male striker will be awarded bonus runs for hitting the ball into the netting zones only if he and his partner complete a run. The six net in mixed games is the same as the other zones in that a batter, either male or female, may be given out caught off the six net after a direct hit.

Male players in mixed competitions may not take advantage of female strikers by bowling too short or too fast. If this happens the umpire may call a no-ball and in doing so the batting side automatically receives two runs.

The rule which applies to field placements in mixed games is also designed so that the male players do not take advantage of the females. The ICS rules state that there must be two females and two males in each half of the court prior to the ball being bowled. If this is not the case, a penalty of five runs is awarded to the batting side.

COMPETITION

Within all stadia, regardless of their company affiliation, indoor cricket is organised on a league basis. Teams are graded according to their ability and slotted into leagues of eight. Each team plays the other teams in the league twice over a period of fourteen weeks. The league season lasts for sixteen weeks and in the last two weeks semi-finals and the grand finals are organised. Teams strive to get into the top four positions in their league in order to have a chance of playing in the finals.

League games can be very tense and competitive. League points are awarded in all league games and these vary according to the stadium. ICS, for example, award four points for a win, one point for every 25 runs scored and one point for every five wickets taken. In the event of a tie, each team receives two points plus the relevant batting and bowling points. Seven points are awarded for a forfeited game. By contrast, Redball award four points for a win and one bonus batting point for every 20 runs scored and a bonus bowling point for every five wickets taken. ICA's system is again very similar in that four points are awarded for a win, one point for every 25 runs scored and one point for every multiple of minus 25 runs a team effects against the opposition. (Yes, in indoor cricket a batting side's total can be a minus quantity!) CBC's system is the same.

PENALTIES

Penalties are awarded by the umpire for any misconduct. Any swearing, arguing with the umpire, undue rough play, unfair play, mistreatment of equipment or undue time-wasting may incur a penalty. This is normally a five-run penalty but the umpire is at liberty to give a more severe penalty if it is fitting. No warning is necessary, and if the misconduct continues the umpire may send off the offending player and at the same time inflict further penalty runs. If these actions escalate to a point where the game has ceased to be under control, the umpire has the right to stop the game and the non-offending side will automatically be awarded seven league points.

The penalties that are incurred are deducted at the time of the offence from the team's batting score. It is the umpire who is solely responsible for the judgement of fair and unfair play. The umpire has the right to intervene without appeal in the event of unfair play and during that time the ball is deemed to be dead. Having said that, it is the responsibility of the captain of the side to ensure that play is conducted within the spirit of the games and the rules at all times.

The ICS rules state, as previously mentioned, that the fielder has right of way if fielding the ball and that a batter may be given out if he interferes with this, but if the umpire considers that any member of the fielding side deliberately obstructs either batter whilst they are attempting to gain their ground, the umpire may penalise the fielding side five runs which will be added to the batter's score. If this occurs and runs are scored by the batting team, those runs will count. Furthermore the umpire will not allow a dismissal on that delivery.

Redball, ICA and CBC rules have penalties awarded for non-conforming uniform. Each member of the team must wear matching coloured tops and the penalty for not doing so is five runs per player. Furthermore no player shall play in jeans or bare feet or leather-soled shoes, a five-run penalty being awarded for each offending item. These points also appear in the ICS rules.

The fielder has deliberately moved across the path of the batter and has no intention of fielding the ball.

Since teams are strictly graded into leagues according to ability, they are sure of enjoyable games with opposition of equal strength. ICS and CBC state that players are not allowed to play in more than one team in the same league in the same competition. But a player is allowed to register for and play in another league team in a different grade. Both the ICA and ICS rules give a penalty of two runs per grade for a player who fills in for a team in a grade lower than that in which he normally plays. There is, however, no penalty for a player filling in for a side in a grade higher than that in which he normally plays.

In most stadia, knock-out competitions are also organised. These can take the form of a straight knock-out, a league cup or a handicapped tournament. In the latter, teams are handicapped according to their grade.

3
Techniques

Since indoor cricket derived initially from the traditional game, many of the techniques transfer directly from traditional cricket. But indoor cricket is faster and is played in an enclosed area, so the basic techniques have adapted to the specific requirements of the indoor game. Many books have already been written which deal with cricket technique and the purpose of this chapter is not to duplicate those, but rather to outline the basics and describe how these can best be used for indoor cricket.

In this chapter, each of the techniques of the game will be dealt with in detail so that the reader can play to the highest level or just get the maximum enjoyment from this fun game, according to his ability. All the techniques mentioned will be for a right-handed player unless otherwise indicated.

The basic overarm bowling grip.

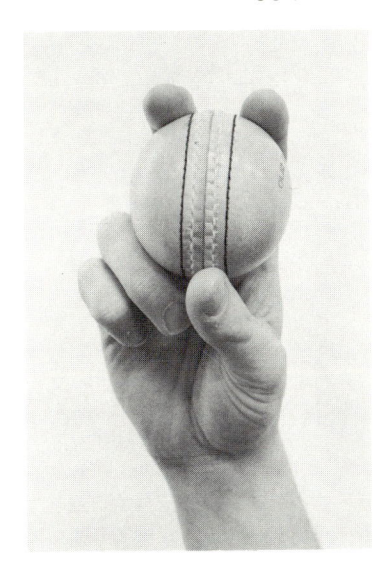

OVERARM BOWLING

Although the overarm bowling techniques in indoor cricket can be equated with those of the traditional game, new underarm techniques have developed which are specific to indoor cricket and these will be dealt with in detail later in this section.

The basic overarm bowling action

The basic grip is shown in the photograph below. It does, however, vary according to the type of delivery that is being bowled. The point common to all types of bowling is that the ball is held in the fingers and not in the palm of the hand, which gives the bowler full control of the delivery.

The basic action is shown in the photographs below. There are slight variations according to the type of delivery that is being bowled.

With the type of ball used and the synthetic surface on which

The basic overarm bowling action. The left arm is stretching up. The head, looking down the wicket, is behind the left arm and steady. The hand holding the ball is near the face. The left shoulder is pointing at the batter and the left arm is stretching up. The right arm begins its downward delivery swing and the body becomes slightly arched. The right foot is parallel to the crease. The bowling arm is high, the left arm swings down and close to the left side, and at the same time the weight is transferred on to the left foot. The follow-through involves the left arm being swung back up behind the body, while the right arm swings down across a braced left leg as it 'chases' the left arm. The head remains balanced, the eyes being level and pointing down the line of the delivery. The body has pivoted, bringing the right shoulder to point at the batter. The right leg is picked up and is brought through close to the left.

The bowler approaching the wicket.

A good sideways position.

The front foot is pointing down the wicket.

The bowler's left leg is braced and she is looking straight down the wicket.

The follow-through.

The basic action from sideways on.

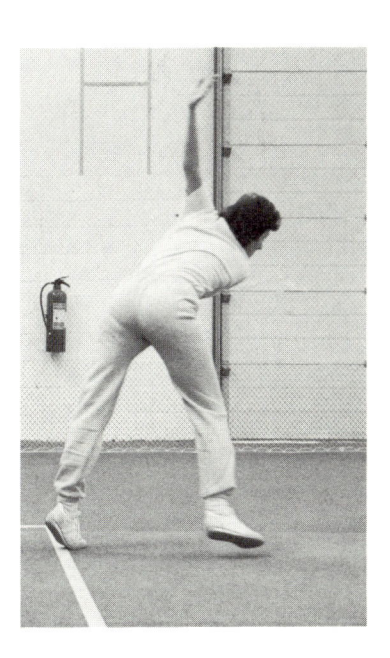

the game is played, many of the top players in Australia and England have found that a spin attack is very effective. Indeed, many of the top players are concentrating on spin attack, at the same time being able to adjust to any situation. The synthetic surface is definitely receptive to spin; the ball bounces quite high and turns appreciably which makes it difficult for the batter to drive.

The objective of the spin-bowler is to deceive the batsman. This can be done by varying the flight of the ball or changing the pace of the delivery, as well as by the degree of turn off the pitch. This will further be dealt with in the chapter on tactics.

Off-spin
The off-spin bowler requires a good basic action and pivot. The wrist of the bowling hand is bent towards the thumb side so that at the bottom of the delivery swing the palm will be facing upwards. It is the fingers and wrist which impart the spin by twisting in a clockwise direction as the ball is delivered; they then continue down across the body during the follow-through.

As a result, the ball will react as illustrated below. The ball will spin from the off stump towards the leg stump, and on the synthetic surface this often gets a great deal of lift.

The alternative delivery to the off-spin is the floater. As its name suggests, this is the ball that, instead of spinning in towards the batter, drifts away from him. From the striking batter's end the grip looks similar to that adopted for the normal off-spin delivery, and because the action is similar the batter can often be deceived into thinking that the ball will spin in towards the stumps. In fact, because the fingers and wrists are kept still, it drifts away from the batter.

Leg-spin
The ball that has the totally opposite effect to the off-spin delivery is the leg-break. The basic delivery for the leg-spin bowler is the ball that will pitch on middle or middle and leg stump and spin towards the off-side.

The leg-break bowler also requires a good basic action, but the action of the wrist and fingers differs in this method of bowling. In this delivery the wrist is bent inwards towards the forearm; it then rotates outwards, with the little finger leading. During the action, as the bowling arm approaches its highest point, the wrist begins to flip forwards in the direction of the striking batter. The third finger also flicks outwards and downwards and this imparts anti-clockwise spin to the ball,

The off-spin grip.

The flight of off-spin.

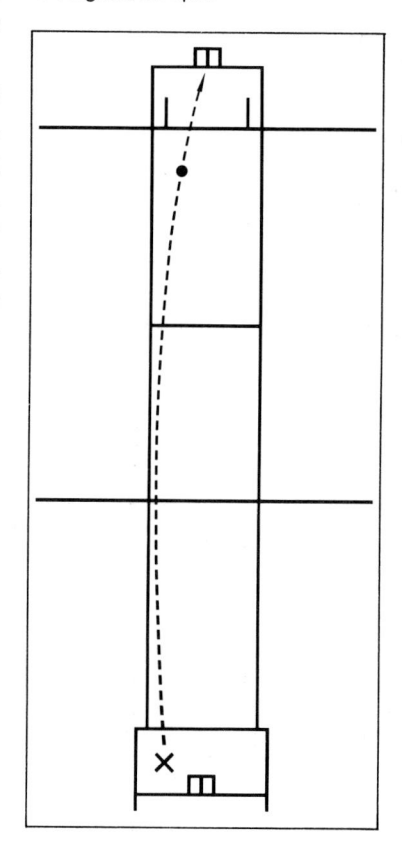

The leg-spin grip.

The flight of leg-spin.

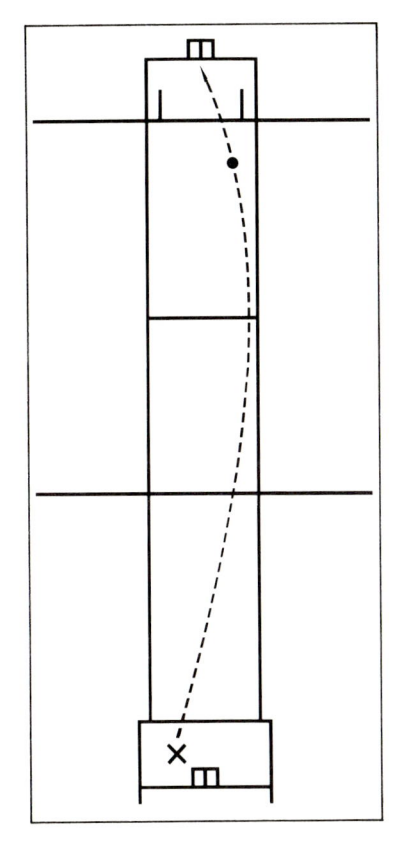

which causes the ball to spin towards the off-side.

The variations to the basic leg-spin delivery are the googly and the top-spinner. The grip for these is the same as for the basic leg-spin delivery. In the leg-break, spin is in an anti-clockwise direction from the leg stump to the off stump, but the googly, which is bowled with almost the same action except that the wrist rotates earlier so that the ball can be felt leaving the hand over the third and little fingers, results in the ball spinning in a clockwise direction from the off stump towards the leg stump.

The top-spinner imparts spin down the line of the flight of the ball so that the ball spins towards the stumps. Again, it is bowled by rotating the wrist slightly earlier than for the leg-break. It is a very difficult ball to bowl as the tendency is for the ball to deviate either to the leg or to the off after pitching.

The left-arm spin-bowler
The grip for the orthodox left-arm spin-bowler is the same as that for the right-arm off-spin bowler, the action also being the same. The effect of this will however be opposite, in that the ball will spin towards the off-side of a right-handed batsman.

The alternative ball will be the 'arm ball', which is the delivery which will drift in towards the right-handed batter, bowled with the same grip as the floater for the right-arm off-spin bowler.

Out-swing
Although spin-bowling is without a doubt an extremely effective means of bowling in indoor cricket, equally as effective, especially with a new ball, is swing-bowling. Two methods of swing-bowling which transfer directly from traditional cricket are out-swing and in-swing.

Out-swing describes a delivery which moves in the air towards the off-side, away from the right-handed batter. For swing-bowling it is vital that the ball is held in the fingers. For the out-swing delivery the seam should be canting past the off stump in the direction of where first slip would be standing in the traditional game. A good basic action is required to perfect this delivery, with the slight modifications that the left shoulder will rotate a bit more. This delivery is bowled with a high arm-action, with the fingers behind the ball and the wrist firm. All this aids the late movement of the ball away from the batter. It is vital for this delivery that there is a good body pivot and a strong follow-through.

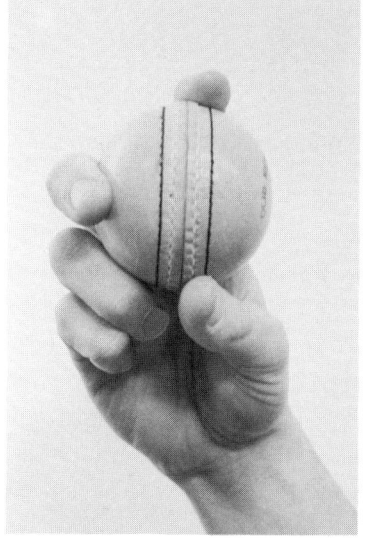

The out-swing grip.   The off-cutter grip.

As with spin-bowling, there is a variation to this basic delivery, called the off-cutter. This ball will move in off the pitch towards the batter and is bowled with basically the same action as the out-swing delivery. The action varies slightly from the out-swing delivery in that the first finger pulls down the seam, which imparts a clockwise spin on the ball.

The planned flight of out-swing.

In-swing

This is the ball which, during its flight, moves in the air in towards the leg stump of the batter. For in-swing bowling the ball is held so that the seam is vertical and points past the leg stump of the batter to where fine-leg would be in the traditional game.

The action for this delivery differs from the basic action in that the bowler becomes more chest-on to the batter. This means that the front foot will be placed more towards the off-side and the head will be inside the left arm, not looking behind it. For this type of delivery the ball is bowled from as high as possible and because of the chest-on nature of the delivery, the bowling arm in the follow-through may come down past the right side of the body.

The leg-cutter is the variation in delivery used by the in-swing bowler. As the ball is delivered, the second finger pulls down across the seam; the thumb pushes and the wrist rotates slightly. This imparts anti-clockwise spin on the ball, making

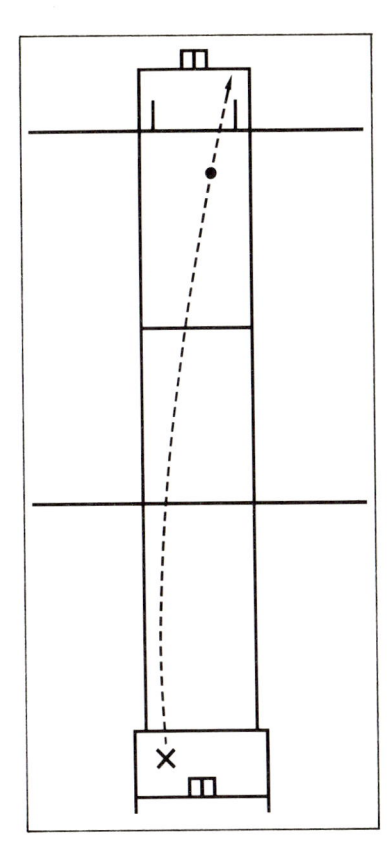

The planned flight of in-swing.

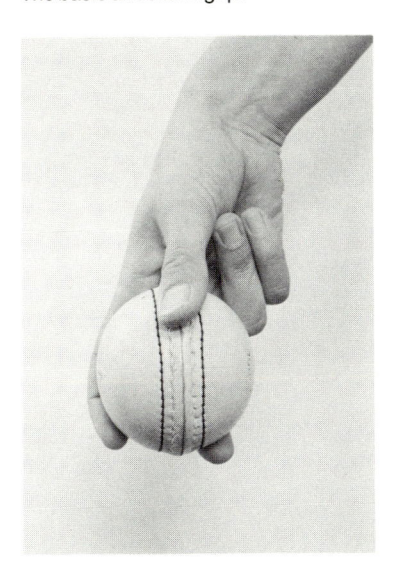

The basic underarm grip.

The in-swing grip.

The leg-cutter grip.

the ball move from the leg-side to the off-side as it strikes the pitch.

The medium-paced bowler needs to rely upon change of pace to deceive the batter. This can be done not only by bowling the 'cutters' as described earlier, but also by bowling a conventional slower ball. This slower delivery can be achieved by holding the ball back, more in the palm of the hand, and bowling in exactly the same way as for the basic delivery.

UNDERARM BOWLING

Many people who play indoor cricket have never played the traditional game. For this reason some players have adopted the underarm method of bowling, and it has in fact become very effective. Many different techniques have developed and the spin-bowling techniques described for the overarm bowler can be even more effective for the underarm bowler.

The underarm action

The ball should be held in the fingers, which gives better control. Some players make the mistake of gripping the ball too far into the palm of the hand, which causes the ball to be released at the wrong time except when the technique has been developed to advantage by the experienced bowler to deliver a slower ball.

The basic underarm action.

Far left: The start of the underarm action.

Left: The underarm follow-through.

The basic underarm action from sideways on.

Preparation.

Beginning the action.

The follow-through.

In order to develop this to a faster delivery, a smooth, rhythmic run-up can be added. Starting by facing the direction in which the ball is to be bowled, the first step is taken onto the left foot, the right foot then passes the left foot with the right foot being brought parallel to the crease, bringing the body into a sideways position ready to bowl the ball as described previously.

Variations of underarm bowling

Simply by delaying the release of the ball, the trajectory of the delivery will become higher. This may well tempt the batter into coming down the wicket and hence provide a possible stumping possibility.

By holding the ball in the palm of the hand and, as with the overarm bowler, using the same basic action, a well-disguised slower ball can be bowled.

Off-spin, leg-spin and top-spin can easily be imparted with an underarm action using similar grips to those described for overarm bowling.

For the off-spin delivery the hand is turned in a clockwise direction on release of the ball, dragging the forefinger over the top of the ball and the seam, thus imparting the anti-clockwise spin. This delivery should be aimed outside the off stump in order to spin the ball back in towards the batter.

An alternative grip used to bowl this ball underarm is by using the thumb. As the ball is released, the thumb rotates over

The grip for the slower ball.

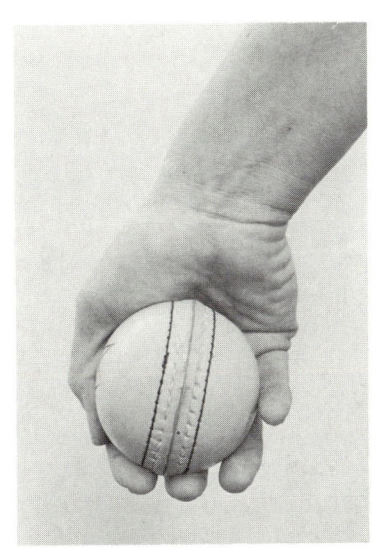

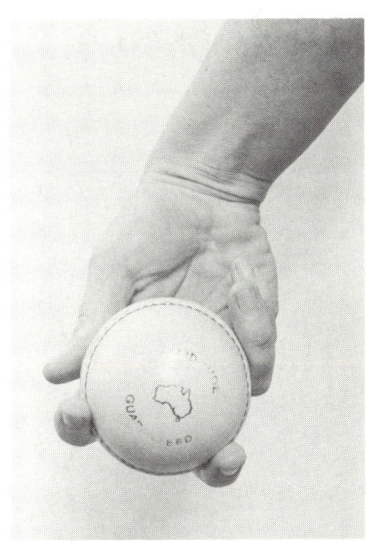

The underarm off-spin grip.

the ball and imparts clockwise spin on the ball. With both of these techniques the palm of the hand will be facing upwards at the completion of the delivery.

The grip for the underarm leg-spin delivery is the same as that for the overarm delivery. On release of the ball, the hand turns in an anti-clockwise direction with the third finger imparting anti-clockwise spin on the ball. On the follow-through the palm of the hand will be facing outwards.

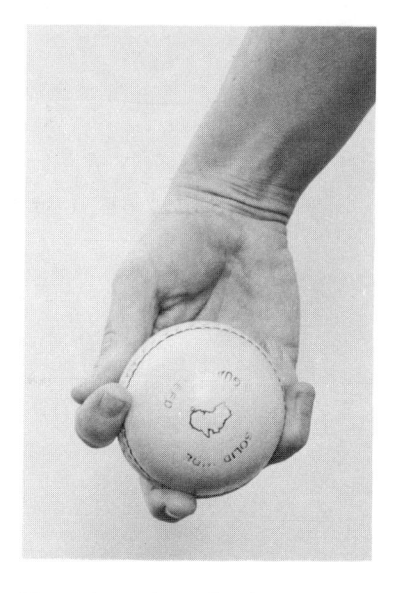

Left-arm underarm bowler
The techniques described for the right-arm bowler are exactly the same for the left-arm bowler. The only difference will be that of spin. The orthodox left-arm spinner, as mentioned in the section on overarm techniques, will grip the ball as the right-arm off-spinner but with the result that the ball will spin away to the off-side.

The underarm leg-spin grip.

Line and length
Any bowler, whether bowling inside or outside, overarm or underarm, must have an understanding of the term 'length' when applied to bowling. As in outdoor cricket, a good-length ball limits the scoring opportunities of the batter, in that it becomes difficult for him to play either back or forwards comfortably.

Taking this a stage further, anything which pitches closer to the batter will enable him to drive the ball. Conversely, anything which pitches short of a length will give the batter time to move onto the back foot and play a forcing shot from there. It must, however, be remembered that a good length for a faster bowler may well differ from a good length for a spin-bowler; the position and height of the batter will also be important factors.

Allied with good length is understanding of 'line', that is the direction of the delivery. The margin of error in indoor cricket outside the leg stump is very narrow, so in order not to incur a two-run penalty the bowler must bowl either straight or just outside the off stump. A more detailed appreciation of line and length will be dealt with in the chapter concerned with tactics.

Both overarm and underarm bowlers have the option of bowling either 'over' or 'round' the wicket, which may be used to tactical advantage. Remember that the umpire must be informed of any change so as not to incur a two-run penalty for bowling a no-ball.

BATTING

The basic batting techniques will, in their correct form, transfer directly from traditional cricket, although it will be seen that modifications are made. Generally speaking, in indoor cricket there is no necessity to hit the ball hard but the emphasis is very much on placement of the ball.

Grip and stance

The overriding factor should be that the batter is comfortable and therefore confident in his position at the crease. The majority of players assume the orthodox stance of the traditional cricketer, a sideways position to the bowler.

The bat should become part of the batter's body in that he feels totally at ease and comfortable with the bat in hand. The 'correct' grip will be as for traditional cricket: the left hand is at the top of the bat and the right hand immediately beneath it (the reverse for a left-hander), so that both hands are close together.

For safety reasons batters are required to wear gloves, as outlined in the chapter on rules, which enable the batter to grip the bat firmly and not endanger the fielders.

For the majority of shots played in indoor cricket, as in the traditional game, the top hand will do most of the work with the

The correct batting grip.   With gloves.   Without gloves.

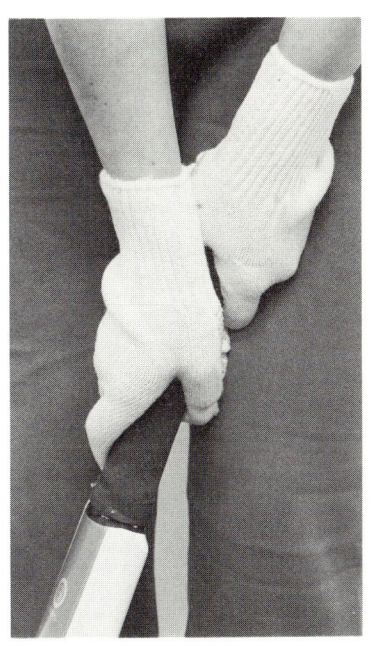

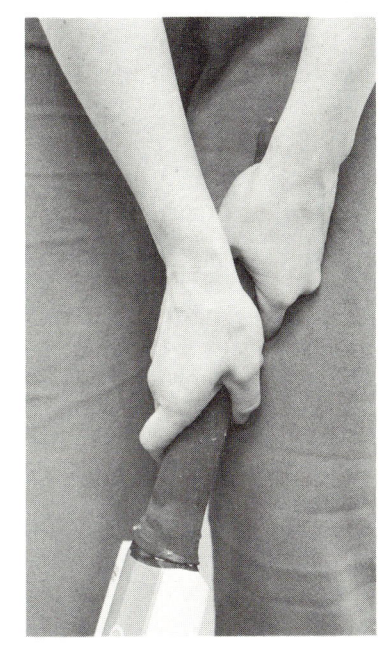

Alternative batting grip.

With gloves.   Without gloves.

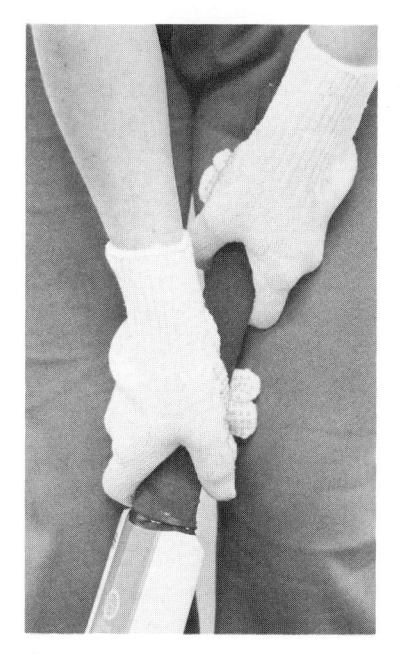

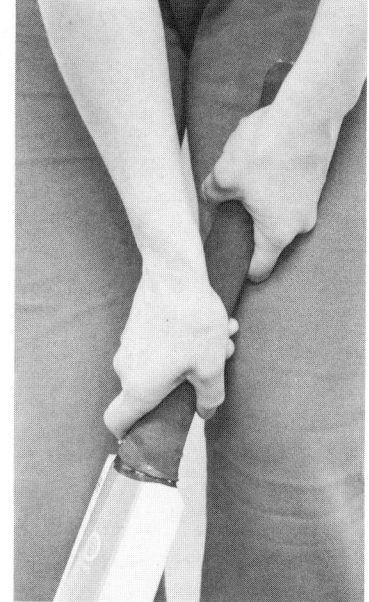

bottom hand working with the top hand to add more power. However, many indoor batters have adopted an alternative grip which allows the bottom hand to become more dominant.

As in the traditional game, the backlift is essential in order to give the batter as much time as possible to make a decision and to play the shot that is required. The bat should be lifted directly back and over middle stump. This should be done with the movement of the arms only so that the batter is able to maintain the sideways position and the eyes are kept still in order to be able to watch the ball. However, many batters will adopt a shorter backlift as they are not required to hit the ball any great distance in the indoor game.

The backlift.

The back-foot forcing shot on the off-side

This shot can be equated with the drive off the back foot in the traditional game, but placement rather than timing becomes all-important. It is played to a short-pitched delivery on or outside the off stump. The batter's first movement should be to take the back foot back, but in line with the ball, the weight being transferred onto the back foot. The back leg should be braced and the bat will be brought through in a vertical position with the full face of the bat making contact with the ball. The follow-through will be in the direction of the intended path of the ball. It is essential throughout this shot that the head is behind the line of the ball and remains still when making contact. The shot is in effect a punch into the off-side.

Forcing the ball into the off-side netting off the back foot.

The back foot is moving back and across in line with the ball.

The head is clearly behind the line and over the ball, and the weight is on the back foot.

The full face of the bat makes contact with the ball. The left elbow is kept high.

The follow-through is in the direction of the ball.

The cut

This shot is more likely to be played to the wider delivery outside the off stump. As in the previous shot, the batter moves onto the back foot, back and across. The bat is then brought down on the ball taking care to roll the wrists, therefore ensuring that the ball is hit down.

The cut.

The back foot is moving across to the off-side. Note that the bat is held high.

The head is still and watching the ball as the bat begins its downward swing.

At the moment of contact with the ball, the wrists have rolled over the top to ensure that the ball is played down.

The follow-through transfers the weight onto the front foot. This ensures that the ball will be hit forward of the batting crease into the scoring zone.

The late cut

This shot is also played off the back foot but is deliberately hit backwards of the batting crease. As before, this shot is played to a short-pitched delivery outside the off stump but the ball is allowed to go beyond the batter and is helped on its way by the batter.

The late cut.

The back foot moves across and into position, the head is still, the eyes are watching the ball, and the bat is held high.

At the moment of contact, the wrists have rolled over the ball. Note that the head is pointing towards the corner of the net, and the eyes are watching the ball.

The bat comes down in the direction of the ball.

The weight, the head and the bat have all finished in the direction in which the ball has been hit.

The checked off-drive

This is played to a well pitched-up ball on or outside the off stump. As in traditional cricket, the first movement is with the head moving in the direction of the ball. At the moment of contact with the ball the head should be over the ball, the front foot next to where the ball has pitched and the weight will be completely on the front foot.

The checked drive.

With bat lifted, the batter is keeping her head steady and is watching the ball.

Her head leads the movement towards where the ball is pitching. Note also that the foot is alongside the ball.

The full face of the bat is making contact with the ball, the head is still down, the weight is on the front foot.

The batter follows through in the direction of the scoring zone, still watching the ball.

The angled bat

It is possible to steer the ball wide of fielders simply by angling the bat at the moment of contact with the ball.

The hit to leg off the back foot

A batter's decision as to which shot to play may be dictated not only by the particular ball that is delivered, but also by the positions of the fielders. Shots normally played to a short-pitched ball outside the off stump have already been dealt with, but should there be a predominantly off-side field, the batter can position himself in order to hit the ball to the leg-side scoring zone. In this case the back foot will move well over to the off-side so that it is outside the line of the ball. The aim will be to hit the ball forward of the batting crease into the scoring zone.

The same shot is played to a short-pitched ball on or outside the leg stump. It is played into the scoring zone by positioning the feet quickly outside the line of the ball once it has been bowled, so that the batter is chest-on to the bowler.

The angled bat. The batter has moved into position as for the off-drive, but at the moment of impact the angled bat steers the ball wide of the fielder.

The pull from outside the off stump.

The batter's stance before the ball is bowled.

The batter has moved chest-on to the bowler, the back foot is outside the line of the ball, the bat is still held high. Note that the feet are positioned so that the ball will be hit forward of the batting crease into the scoring zone.

The bat has come down on the ball, the wrists have rolled, and the weight has transferred onto the front foot.

The hit to leg off the back foot. ◀

The batter, with bat lifted, waits for the delivery.

Her back foot has moved first backwards and outside the line of the ball, with her toe pointing down the wicket, bringing the batter 'chest on'. Note that the bat is still held high.

The leg-drive off the front foot. ▶

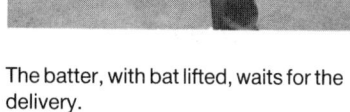

On contact with the ball the weight is transferred onto the front foot and the wrists have 'rolled'.

The follow-through, showing the wrists 'rolled'. The weight is on the front foot, so the ball has been hit downwards.

The hit to the off-side from outside the leg stump. ▶ ▼

The batter in stance, watching the ball.

The leg-drive

This is similar to the checked drive on the front foot on the off-side, but in executing this shot the batter will make an adjustment by simply opening his shoulders as the ball comes towards him.

The batter may decide to hit the ball pitching outside the leg stump to the off-side should there be a predominantly leg-side field.

The batter, watching the ball, is beginning to open her shoulders.

Her head is over the ball, her weight is on the front foot and the full face of the bat has just made contact with the ball.

The follow-through with the full face of the bat in the direction of the ball. The batter's eyes are still watching the ball.

The batter moving back to the leg-side, with her head still and watching the ball. Note that her bat is still held up in position.

The bat is coming down towards the ball to make contact with it. Note that the batter's head is still over the ball.

Her wrists have rolled, ensuring that the ball is hit downwards.

55

The lofted drive

The most difficult scoring zone to reach is Zone D and hitting this target results in the scoring of most runs. The shot most effective in hitting this zone on the full, therefore scoring six runs, is the lofted drive.

The lofted drive.

The batter is in her normal stance, with her bat lifted ready for the delivery.

The contact with the ball is made on the 'up', with the bat facing upwards and following the intended direction of the ball.

The batter is moving down the wicket towards the ball by placing her left foot forward. The right foot passes behind the left as shown, so that the batter maintains a sideways position. It is important that the head is kept still.

The follow-through continues in an upward direction, the weight transferring onto the front foot in the direction in which it is intended that the ball should be hit.

The block and run.

The 'block and run'

This shot is effective when the close fielders are away from the pitch, protecting the netted scoring zones. It is then possible to block the ball and cross for a single.

The batter, with head over the ball, is playing a 'dead' bat to stop the ball at her feet.

The ball is stationary on the pitch and the batter is setting off for a single.

The batter continues to run directly down the wicket.

Running between the wickets

This is a very important part of the game. It is essential to develop a good understanding between each batting partnership. This will not only cut down the number of run-outs but will also keep the batting score ticking over.

The backing-up batter can shorten the distance that he will have to run by standing in the correct position on the running crease.

The backing-up batter will move two or three metres in the direction of the batting crease at each delivery but must always be able to return to the running crease if no run can be taken. As in the traditional game, calling can be used. As a general rule, if the ball is hit backward of the batting crease or simply if the ball is struck wide of the left hand of the fielders on the off-side or wide of the right hand of the fielders on the leg-side, the call will be made by the backing-up batter as he will be running to the danger end. Similarly, if the ball is hit beyond the running crease or simply wide of the right hand of the fielders on the

Note the non-striking batter holding the bat in his left hand. His body faces in the direction of the intended run, but his head is clearly facing the bowler as he waits for the ball to be released before leaving the running crease.

off-side or wide of the left hand of the fielders on the leg-side, the call will be made by the striking batter, as he will be running to the danger end. As a greater understanding is developed between batting pairs, they may well dispense with calling and simply be able to communicate by a nod of the head for example. This understanding can be developed to such an extent that it almost seems like telepathy.

The difference between being in and being out on a run-out can simply be the grounding and sliding of the bat across the line.

Sliding the bat.

The batter has grounded her bat on its edge and is reaching for the line.

She continues to sprint and reach, her arm outstretched.

Sliding the bat (continued).
She is home safely, her grounded bat having crossed the line.

The technique shown in the photographs above applies when a batter is sprinting for a quick single, but should he be looking for a second run, the bat should be grounded behind the line (or just in front of it and slid in) so that he is in position for a second run, as in the photographs below.

Returning for a second run.

The batter is about to slide her bat behind the line and look for a second run.

Having seen the opportunity she is able to return quickly in the opposite direction for a second run.

59

FIELDING

The game of indoor cricket provides many and varied opportunities where fielding skills are all-important. The traditional cricketer will use the game to sharpen up and improve his close-fielding techniques for the outdoor game. Those people who play only indoor cricket will see the need to improve and perfect their fielding skills simply to be good at indoor cricket. Having said this, the techniques used are very similar to those employed in the traditional game. Most fielding techniques will be essentially attacking, due to the nature of the game.

Fielding in the front section of the court

The close-catching position is shown below. Catches may be taken having rebounded from the roof or side netting, so the fielder may position himself at a slight angle.

The fielder has his hands ready, with fingers spread and little fingers together. The fielder's weight is forwards on the balls of his feet, his knees are slightly bent, his head is still, and his eyes are keenly watching the ball leaving the bat. Concentration is all-important to be able to take sharp chances.

The fielder is slightly turned outwards towards the netting, in the stance described in the previous photo, but with his head clearly turned in the direction of the batter in anticipation of the shot.

Ground-fielding close to the wicket

The aim when fielding the ball on the ground close to the wicket is to return it to the stumps either into the hands of the wicketkeeper or as a direct hit for a run-out.

In executing this skill it is essential that the fielder maintains a low position and that the ball is transferred from the hands to the stumps as quickly as possible.

Ground-fielding close to the wicket.

The fielder is receiving the ball with his hand behind the ball, his fingers outstretched and his head over the ball. He is keeping a low position.

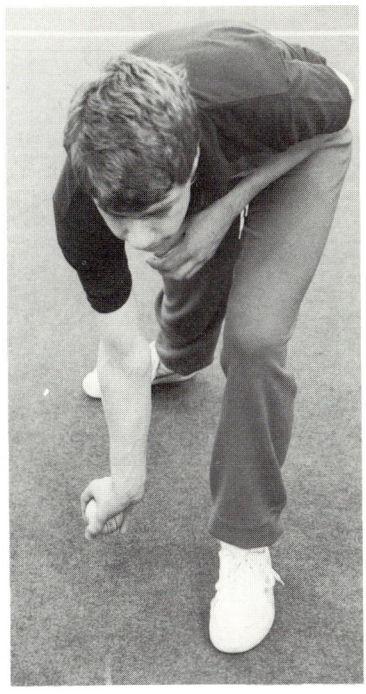

With his ball in his hand and his wrist cocked backwards, the fielder's eyes are intent on the wicket.

The fielder's hand flicks the ball in the direction of the stumps, while his weight and follow-through continue in that direction.

Chase, turn and throw

A run-out opportunity may present itself which requires the fielder to chase, turn and throw the ball.

Chase, turn and throw.

Having chased the ball, the fielder is picking it up with her right foot alongside the ball and her hand in front of the ball so that it will roll into it. Her head is clearly over the ball and her weight on the front leg.

Chase, turn and throw (continued).

The fielder has turned to her left, with her weight still on the back foot. Her throwing arm is in position ready to release the ball, and her non-throwing arm is outstretched in the direction of the target.

The weight has been transferred onto the front leg, the ball has been released and the follow-through of the throwing arm is in the direction of the target.

Fielding at the back of the court

Many of the skills already described will be used at the back of the court. However, the fielders at the back of the court are protecting the highest-scoring zone, so there will be a need for defensive fielding in order to be sure that a four is not scored. The long barrier is one such technique, which enables the fielder to stop the ball along the ground with the added security that his body is behind his hands. He goes down on his left knee, with his lower left leg forming a line at right angles to the path of the ball as it comes towards him. His right heel is against his left knee and his right leg continues the line of his lower left leg, making one long barrier. His hands field the ball in front of his left knee. From this position he can simply take one step to throw the ball to either end.

There will be times when the fielder will need to prevent the ball hitting a scoring zone by the quickest means possible. This can be done with either an outstretched hand or foot.

Hand and foot stops.

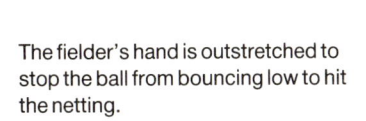

The fielder's hand is outstretched to stop the ball from bouncing low to hit the netting.

The fielder's hand is outstretched to prevent the ball from bouncing higher to hit the netting.

The fielder's foot is outstretched to prevent the ball from hitting the netting along the ground.

Diving to take a catch
Fielders should develop the techniques of diving not only to be able to hold a catch but also to be able to protect themselves. In the sequence of photographs the fielder is seen taking the catch and rolling over to his right side to protect himself.

Diving techniques.

Diving techniques (continued).

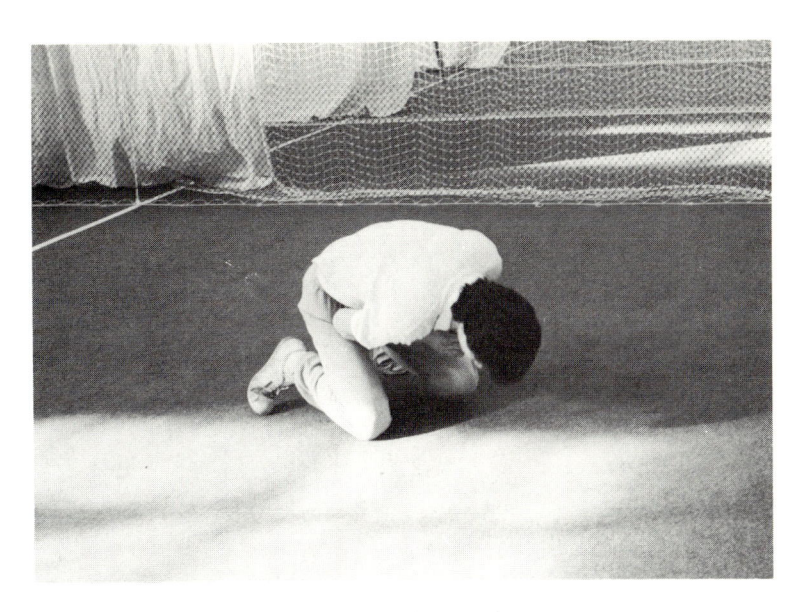

Wicketkeeping

There are two basic positions which indoor cricket wicketkeepers tend to adopt. These are shown in the photographs.

Wicketkeeping.

The wicketkeeper is down with his left foot in line with the middle and off stumps, his weight is on the balls of his feet and his hands are together, waiting to receive the ball.

The wicketkeeper is more upright, but with his weight still on the balls of his feet. His hands are in position level with the top of the stumps, ready to receive the ball.

Off-side stumping

When attempting a stumping, speed is all-important in getting the ball into the gloves and removing the bails as quickly as possible. The technique involved in this is clearly shown in the following photographs.

The sequence shown above is to a particularly wide delivery outside the off stump, making the task of gathering the ball and removing the bails that much more difficult.

An off-side stumping.

The wicketkeeper is moving his right foot across so that it is in line with the ball, as are his hands and head.

The ball has been securely gathered and the wicketkeeper is transferring his weight back to the stumps. Note that his eyes are watching the stumps.

The ball is entering the wicketkeeper's outstretched hands. Note that his left foot is still in position between the middle and off stumps, ready to bring the ball back to the stumps.

The bails have been removed in one action.

Leg-side stumping

A leg-side stumping is probably the most difficult because in moving across to the leg-side the wicketkeeper will momentarily become unsighted, so he will have to anticipate where to receive the ball.

In indoor cricket it is essential that the wicketkeeper is very mobile and is able to field the ball in the area behind the batting crease. Therefore some wicketkeepers prefer to use only one

A leg-side stumping.

The wicketkeeper is moving across to the leg-side to receive the ball.

The ball is entering the wicketkeeper's outstretched hands. Note the positions of his head and feet.

The ball has been gathered, and the weight is transferred back in the direction of the stumps.

The bails have been removed in one action.

67

glove so that they have a hand free to field the ball and throw it at the stumps for a run-out at either end. Some teams dispense with a wicketkeeper altogether, but in doing this they are excluding the opportunities of catches and stumpings normally taken by the wicketkeeper.

4
Tactics

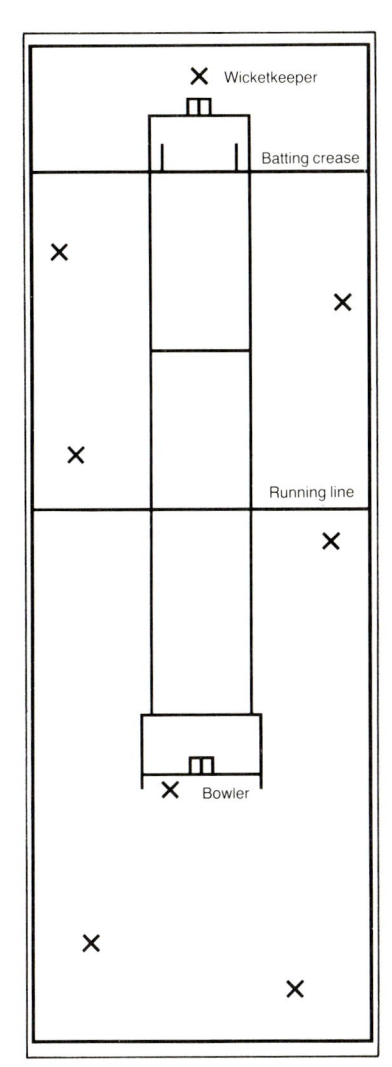

A basic field-placing.

As in all competitive games, when the teams or individuals have acquired the skills and the techniques necessary, the next step is to develop a means of using these to gain the best possible results. Indoor cricket is a relatively new game in which theories are being developed in many different directions. These ideas are called tactics. There are numerous situations within a game which will challenge a team into devising a tactic which will control their own destiny. In this chapter many of the situations which occur in indoor cricket will be identified.

TACTICS FOR THE FIELDING TEAM

The basic field-placing

All the tactics described are based on a right-handed bowler and a right-handed batter unless otherwise indicated.

When teams first play indoor cricket, their main concern will be to defend the high-scoring zones. The rules dictate that there must be four fielders in each half of the court, so it is likely that the captain will place the field in a similar fashion to that shown above. The diagram shows a wicketkeeper in position behind the stumps, two fielders close to the net on the off-side, one on the leg-side, in the front half of the court. The back half of the court has the bowler about to deliver the ball, a fielder on the leg-side just behind the running crease and two fielders protecting the highest-scoring back net.

This field-placing will make it difficult for the batter to score against the netting, but will allow singles to be run. It will vary as shown below if the batter is unlikely to be strong enough to score by hitting the back net for a four or a six. In this case there is only one fielder protecting the back net, the other fielder having moved up to the running crease.

The decision whether to place more fielders on the off-side or the leg-side will depend on two factors. The first of these is the type of bowling and the second the technique of the striking batter.

The out-swing bowler will demand a more predominantly off-side field as the ball will be moving away from the right-handed batter. By contrast, the in-swing bowler will require more fielders on the leg-side as the ball is moving in towards the right-handed batter, and therefore towards the leg-side. However, if the batter's techniques indicate that he will mainly hit the ball to the leg-side, even the away-swing bowler may nullify this by placing an extra fielder on the leg-side. This is a common trait as many batters naturally use more bottom hand in their shots. Similarly, but less frequent, if a batter naturally hits the ball to the off-side, even the in-swing bowler may place an extra fielder on the off-side to decrease scoring opportunities.

For the slow and spin-bowler it may be necessary to place more emphasis on defending the four/six net as many batters will attempt to hit the bowler over his head. However, a good spin-bowler will be able to prevent this by altering the trajectory of the ball, by varying the pace. The competent off-spin bowler will therefore have more fielders on the leg-side as the ball will be moving in that direction. Similarly, the leg-spin bowler will have more fielders on the off-side as the ball will be turning in that direction. Again, the technique of the batter will influence the field-placing.

These field placings will apply to both the underarm and overarm bowler.

A more attacking field-placing.

Fielders in close-catching positions. Note that there are two on the leg-side, so the bowler is likely to be an off-spinner.

Attacking field-placing

The taking of wickets in indoor cricket inflicts a five-run deficit on the batting team, so the fielding side will want to place their field in such a way as to increase their wicket-taking opportunities. Pressure can be applied to the batter by placing fielders in close-catching positions.

A fielder moving from the back court into the front court as the ball is on its way down the pitch, to help cut down the scoring opportunities in this area.

71

The fielding side is limited to the number of fielders allowed either side of the running crease, but a fielder may move from the back half of the court over the running crease or vice versa as soon as the ball is released by the bowler. This tactic may be used for two purposes. Firstly, the fielder may move into the front half of the court to increase the pressure on the batter in order to take wickets. Secondly, if the batters are scoring their runs predominantly in the front half of the court the additional fielder will assist in preventing their scoring opportunities. This can be taken a stage further by more than one fielder moving from one half of the court into the other.

Teams may wish to adopt the tactic of foregoing the wicketkeeper in order to increase the number of close fielders in front of the bat. In this instance it is vital that the bowler forces the batter to play the ball by bowling straight, or he will simply allow it to pass by, knowing that the ball will not hit the wickets and that he cannot be caught or stumped by a wicketkeeper.

If the batters are employing a 'block and run' tactic the fielding team can position a fielder very straight, though not on the pitch, to combat this and also to provide the opportunities for run-outs.

All four fielders are in front of the bat and there is no wicketkeeper.

Defensive field-placing

The basic field-placing already described can be used as a defensive tactic. This could be employed if the batting team requires a large number of runs in their last overs, so the fielding team will be content to allow singles but cannot afford the high-scoring areas to be penetrated. In this situation, fielders may move from the front half of the court to the back half of the court as the ball is released by the bowler, thus giving added protection to the high-scoring zones: two, four and six runs. The bowler can help by bowling short of a length, thus making it difficult for the batter to drive.

The best means of defence is for the bowler to be able to bowl to his field. However, a ball that is difficult to score from is a fast full toss bowled at waist-height to the batter.

Bowling order

Prior knowledge of the batting line-up of the opposition is a great advantage to the fielding captain when he is devising his tactics, especially when it comes to planning how to make use of his bowlers. If a team has eight good bowlers this does not create a problem. However, teams are usually made up of a wider range of types of bowler of varying ability. Depending on the opposition's batting line-up, it is customary to use the better bowlers during the first four overs and the last four overs of their innings. However, it could be to the fielding team's advantage to use one of their better bowlers against the weaker batters in order to take wickets.

Safety tactics

The 'live ball' rule peculiar to this game requires the fielding team to take great care at all times to minimise the opportunities of the batters to steal extra runs. The most obvious of these is when the bowler returns to his starting position for the next delivery. The fielding team should relay the ball to a fielder in position behind the stumps at the bowler's end while the bowler takes up his position. This fielder must be able to throw the ball accurately to the striking batter's end should the batters attempt to steal a run by the striker running to the running

The ball is being thrown accurately into the wicketkeeper's gloves for a run-out.

crease before the non-striker leaves it. Should an easy run-out opportunity present itself the fielder should throw the ball accurately to either the wicketkeeper or the fielder at the stumps at the bowler's end. A direct hit on the wicket is not necessary.

In some instances the wicketkeeper and bowler will have been drawn out of position and a run-out cannot be achieved unless there is a direct hit on the stumps. In this situation another fielder must position himself to be able to take the ball safely should it miss or rebound awkwardly. This is essential to prevent the batters taking an extra run. Fielders should automatically position themselves to 'back up' the stumps whether or not their team-mate with the ball attempts a run-out.

Fielders in the front half of the court should have quick reactions and be able to move off in any direction at speed. Those in the back half of the court should be able to position themselves behind the ball either to take a catch or simply to prevent the ball hitting the net. A captain will position his players according to their abilities. In the mixed competitions this is also dictated by the rules but the same principle will apply.

TACTICS FOR THE BATTING TEAM

The way in which the batting team approaches their innings will depend upon several factors. If they are batting first then they will be looking to accumulate the highest score possible and a gradual build-up through the innings is the best way to achieve this. If a team is batting second their batting tactics will be influenced by the total that they are chasing.

The bonus-point system will also give an added incentive to teams whether they win or lose, but a close-fought match with the team batting second already past the opposition's score will often see them batting defensively in order to safeguard their victory.

A team chasing a low score will often adopt the approach of scoring by hitting into the netted scoring zones rather than attempting any runs. This eliminates the possibility of being run out.

The batters may alter their approach according to the opposition's field-placings. If the back net is left vulnerable by having only one fielder protecting it, the batters may attempt to score their runs by forcing the ball hard towards the back net.

The backing-up batter is almost at the batting crease before the striking batter leaves.

If the fielding team have a predominantly off-side field, the batters should attempt to force the ball to the leg-side. Similarly, if the fielding team has a predominantly leg-side field the ball should be forced to the off-side.

If the fielders are in defensive positions away from the batter, the batters can adopt the 'block and run' tactic. This involves them stopping the ball dead, and crossing for a single.

The batters may also adopt a relay system of running between wickets, when one batter runs to the other batter's crease before the latter leaves it to run to the other end. By this tactic, the batter running towards the end nearest to wherever the ball is can complete his run before his partner sets off.

Batting order

The most important decision the captain will make is which batters bat together. A good understanding in a partnership is essential. The most productive and efficient batting pairs will be looking to score from each ball. This requires quick and positive decisions and a similar response from the partner.

A team will benefit most from a sound start and an experienced pair to conclude the innings. Generally speaking, the best partnership should bat last, the next best partnership should open the innings.

The opening pair should accumulate runs with as little risk as possible. Wickets lost at this stage put added pressure on the batters to follow. The second and third pairs will gain confidence from a good start and should be able to continue to accumulate runs at the same rate and may even be able to accelerate. The final pair should ideally be versatile in their

75

ability. They should be not only capable of scoring high partnerships but also able to see their team home safely to victory without incurring unnecessary risk. This requires a good temperament, the ability to withstand pressure and the ability to accept the ultimate challenge.

VARIATIONS TO OUTWIT OPPONENTS

The fielding side may need to introduce variations to upset a batting partnership which appears to be scoring freely. Variations of the different type of bowling have already been described, but each bowler has several ways of altering the delivery. The bowlers can change the line that they bowl by either varying their position on the crease or by altering the side of the wicket from which they bowl. The bowlers can of course change from bowling underarm to overarm or vice versa. The bowlers should also vary the pace of the deliveries in order not to allow the batter to become accustomed to one speed of delivery.

The batter can similarly unsettle the fielders by using an angled bat to 'wrong foot' them.

Teams will no doubt develop their own ideas on how to beat their opponents. It is important, however, that these tactics are within the spirit of the game.

5
Training Practices for Indoor Cricket

We have described the rules of the game, the techniques of the skills involved and the tactics that can be implemented to effect a victory, but anyone having played the game will be intent on doing better next time, win or lose.

It is one thing knowing what to do and how to do it, but the ability to do it consistently will depend upon practice. To some people this prospect may sound exceedingly boring and involve unnecessary hard work. However, this need not be the case; at least, the hard work may be there but practice can be fun and enjoyable, particularly when done as a group or team. Not only do the skills improve but the feeling of team spirit can develop at the same time.

As this is a fast, action-packed game and requires people to react quickly and perform skills under pressure, many of the practices described will not only involve repeating skills time and time again but will put the player into a pressure situation, simulating the game itself.

The practices shown took place on a court and obviously this is ideal, but should it not be possible to have access to these facilities, the practices can be organised easily in an area of similar size.

FIELDING PRACTICES

Catching
We may all think that we can catch but the time that we have to react to take a catch is often very short, so the following practices will help to sharpen up reactions.

The pairs line up facing each other, approximately two metres apart, in a close-catching position. The ball is thrown backwards and forwards between the two as quickly as possible. The pairs can be put under pressure by being timed for one minute, counting the number of catches. This introduces competition as each pair strives to make the highest number of catches. This not only warms up the hands but also develops concentration.

Catching off the netting
The pairs are lined up along the netting (or this can also be done against a wall), the feeder standing behind the catcher as shown. The feeder throws the ball against the netting and the fielder has to react quickly to make the catch.

The fielder should be in a close-catching position, ready to move in any direction and watching the netting carefully. The practice can be made more difficult by feeding the ball at different angles and by varying the strength of the throw so that it rebounds in different ways. The degree of difficulty can also be increased by the fielder moving closer to the net.

Practising catches straight from the netting.

Turning to take a catch off the netting

The pairs are lined up in a similar way to the previous practice but the fielder has his back to the netting. The feeder faces the fielder and throws the ball against the netting. The fielder has to run towards the netting and react to take the catch.

Practising turning and taking a catch from the netting.

Taking catches directly from the bat

The fielders form a semi-circle three or four metres from the batter. They should take up close-catching positions and concentrate on the bat. The ball is fed to the batter, who hits the ball at varying angles and strengths to the fielders. This practice should begin by the batter hitting the ball to each fielder in turn. The degree of difficulty can be increased by not hitting in sequence so that the fielders do not know in advance that the ball will be coming to them.

Catching practice direct from the bat.

Taking catches at an angle from the netting
The feeder and the fielder should be positioned approximately ten metres apart and both two metres from the netting. The feeder will throw the ball hard overarm against the netting at an angle, for the fielder to take a catch. The fielder then becomes the feeder and can return the ball in a similar manner so that his partner takes a catch. The ball should be thrown mostly high and hard and the roof netting can even be involved in this. This practice can become competitive by each person counting the number of catches he takes and attempting to beat his partner.

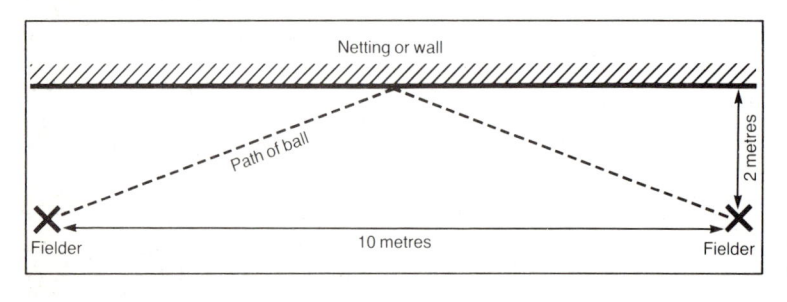

Practising catches at an angle from the netting.

The underarm flick
This technique can be practised in pairs without pressure. However, it will be necessary to see if this skill will stand up in a game situation so the next practice has the fielder competing against a batter.

The feeder is in position next to the stumps and there are two lines of players on the running crease waiting to compete. The fielder and batter are both waiting to sprint the moment that the feeder rolls out the ball. The aim of the fielder is to pick up the ball and make a direct hit to the stumps before the batter makes good his ground.

Competitive practice of the underarm flick.

The feeder is about to roll the ball out.

The fielder has picked up the ball and the batter is halfway.

The fielder has flicked the ball towards the stumps and the batter is beginning to reach out with his bat for the line.

81

Competitive practice of the underarm flick (continued).

The fielder has followed through towards the stumps, the batter is sliding his bat for the line but fortunately for him the fielder has missed the stumps. One point to the batter!

It helps to make this practice fun and perhaps more exciting if a scoring system is introduced. The batters will score one point each time that they get home safely and the fielders will score five points each time that they run the batter out. The two teams can compete against each other for an equal number of turns at both fielding and sprinting for a quick single. The feeder will umpire and award points.

Chase, turn and throw
This practice involves the fielder, who is under pressure, having to turn and throw at the stumps at the bowler's end whilst the batter tries to complete two runs.

The fielder and the batter stand ready to sprint from the running crease. The feeder, from next to the bowler's stumps, rolls the ball out hard towards the batting end. Both the fielder and the batter are facing the batting end and cannot leave the running crease until the ball has crossed it.

Again a scoring system can be introduced to give the practice some extra competition and excitement. The fielder scores five points for a run out and the batter scores two points if he gets home safely. The two teams have an equal number of turns and then change over. This scoring system helps to give an added sense of urgency to the practice. The feeder will 'umpire' all decisions.

Defensive fielding on the back net
Indoor cricket very rarely involves anything which can be called defence because usually it can be very quickly converted into an

Competitive practice of the chase, turn and throw.

The feeder is about to roll the ball past the batter and fielder as they stand ready on the running crease.

The fielder is catching up with the ball as the batter turns for a second run.

The fielder is picking up the ball and turning to throw, the batter is beginning his second run.

Competitive practice of the chase, turn and throw (continued).

The fielder has thrown the ball and the batter is about to reach for the line.

The batter is reaching for the line. Will the ball hit the stumps before he can get there?

attacking move. The back net is the highest-scoring zone and therefore should be protected with great care by the fielder. This means getting the body behind the ball whenever possible. The next practice is to help the fielder change from a defensive position, a long barrier, to an attacking one and hence create a possible run-out opportunity.

A scoring system for this practice could be one point for the fielder stopping the ball, five points for a run-out and one point if the batter gets home safely. The teams have an equal number of turns and then change over, competing against each other for the highest number of points.

Fitness is a very important ingredient in this game and many of the fielding practices not only improve the skills themselves but also assist in producing a fitter team. It is possible to make these practices competitive and fun to the extent where everyone forgets that it is really a form of fitness training!

WICKETKEEPING PRACTICES

The wicketkeeper is not only expected to take catches and stumpings and to assist in run-outs but must also be an agile fielder who patrols the area behind the batting crease to make direct hits at the stumps for run-outs himself.

The wicketkeeper cannot be just one person as all fielders are also bowlers, so all players should be able to do the job.

Fielding for wicketkeepers

The wicketkeeper should always be ready to move to the off-side or to the leg-side. This practice starts with the wicketkeeper behind the stumps and the feeder, armed with several balls, on the underarm line. He rolls the ball wide of the stumps, sometimes to the off-side, sometimes to the leg-side. The wicketkeeper has to field it and throw at the stumps, trying for a run-out.

The feeder is ready to roll the ball out to either side.

Wicketkeeping practice on the off-side.

The wicketkeeper is moving to the off-side, his eyes clearly watching the ball.

85

Wicketkeeping practice on the off-side (continued).

He is receiving the ball with his hands behind it and his head over it.

He is turning and preparing to throw at the stumps.

He follows through towards the stumps.

Stumping

The wicketkeeper not only has the opportunity to run an opponent out but is also able to dismiss the batter, so inflicting a five-run penalty, by catching him out or stumping him out. These too must be practised.

For a stumping, the wicketkeeper should be aiming to receive the ball and remove the bails as quickly as possible. To practise, he will be fed balls continually from five to ten metres away, first down the off-side and then down the leg-side so that he is getting intensive practice at removing the bails. The feeder should vary the length and width of the delivery as the practice progresses.

This practice should be repeated with a batter in position dummying shots, so that the practice reflects the real situation.

Wicketkeeping practice on the leg-side.

The wicketkeeper is moving to the leg-side. Note that he is wearing only one glove.

He is about to receive the ball.

He is picking up the ball and beginning to turn.

Having turned, he is about to throw at the stumps with the ball in the hand without a glove.

The batter should attempt to make good his ground, putting pressure on the wicketkeeper to speed up the action.

Catching for wicketkeepers

The wicketkeeper can not only take catches directly from the bat but also has the opportunity to pick up catches from the back and side netting and should therefore be able to dive.

This practice should be carried out initially using matting or mattresses as a surface on which to dive in order to give the wicketkeeper confidence.

The feeder will be armed with numerous cricket balls so that the wicketkeeper is continually working. The wicketkeeper stands between two diving areas and the ball is fed to either side so that he has to dive to take the catch. He must recover and take up his position quickly, ready for the next catch.

A progression of this practice is to place the diving areas in front of the netting or a wall and the feeder will throw the ball against the net or wall so that it rebounds from it. The wicketkeeper will start facing the feeder and with his back to the netting so that he has to turn and dive to take the rebound.

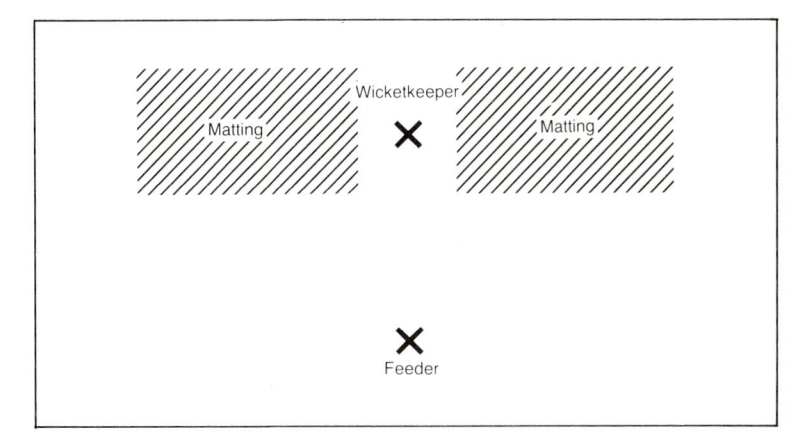

Diving practice for wicketkeepers.

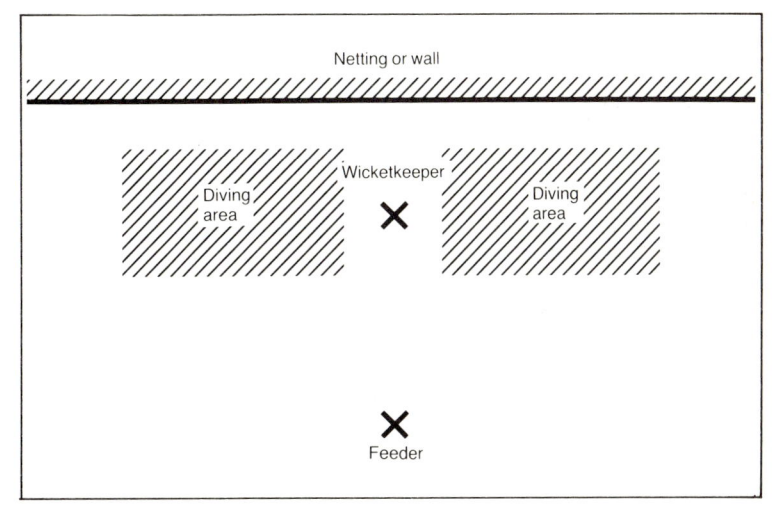

Diving to take catches from the netting.

BATTING PRACTICES

The techniques of all the batting shots can be practised by the individual or in pairs, as is often recommended for the traditional game. However, indoor cricket batting skills are very dependent on placement, so practising this will help a batter to learn the control necessary to hit the ball into a specific area.

The same degree of intensity that was applied to the wicketkeeping skills can be used for batting, so that by repeating the skill over and over again under pressure the batter will feel confident to use it in a game.

89

Placement

The idea of this practice is to challenge the batter to place the ball into specific areas.

The feeder will be armed with numerous cricket balls and the batter will stand in his normal stance. The feeder will throw the balls one after the other outside the off-stump and the batter must try to hit the balls between cones positioned as in the diagram. The feeder must wait until the batter has resumed his stance before throwing.

This practice can be adapted in several ways. First, the feeder can alter where he pitches the ball, including outside the leg-stump, so that the batter must change his shot accordingly. Secondly, the positions of the cones can be changed so that the batter is playing the ball into a different area. The batter can be given the incentive of scoring five runs each time he bisects the cones, thereby introducing an element of competition as each batter has a turn and tries to beat his opponents' score.

This practice can be developed still further by simply putting the cones further apart and placing a fielder between them to defend the scoring zone. The batter now has not only to place the ball but to hit it in such a way that it beats the fielder. The same scoring system can apply but this time the fielder scores one point for every ball he stops and three points for a catch. Again, everyone has a turn at each aspect of this practice and keeps a tally of his own score.

This practice can of course be adapted to the leg-side by placing the cones against the netting on the other side. The cones can also be positioned on the back netting to practise the straight shots.

Weighting

It is important not only to place the ball when batting but to control the pace at which it is hit. This will of course vary according to the situation, but what is important is that the batter 'feels' the weighting of the shot.

This practice is set up in a similar way to the previous one but with three cones in position in a triangle. The first practice is simply for the batter to try to hit the ball hard against the cones to knock them over. The second practice is to try to hit the ball gently so that it settles between the cones, within the triangle. This can be done by hitting the ball gently against the netting so that it rebounds into this area. To start with, the cones should be placed in a large triangle as this practice is very difficult. As the batter becomes more proficient the triangle should be made

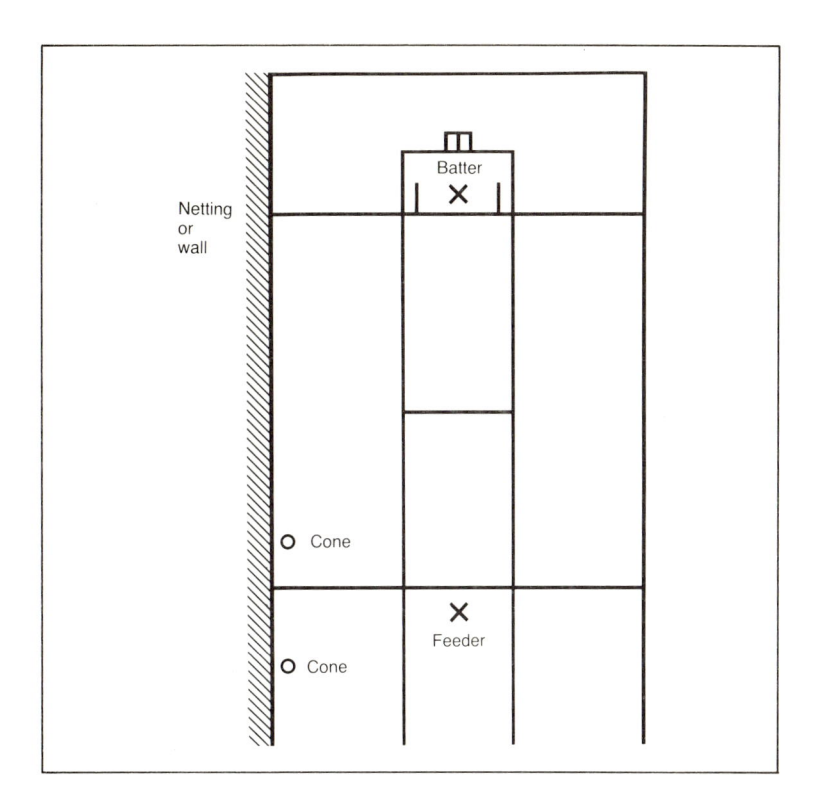

Batting practice – placement.

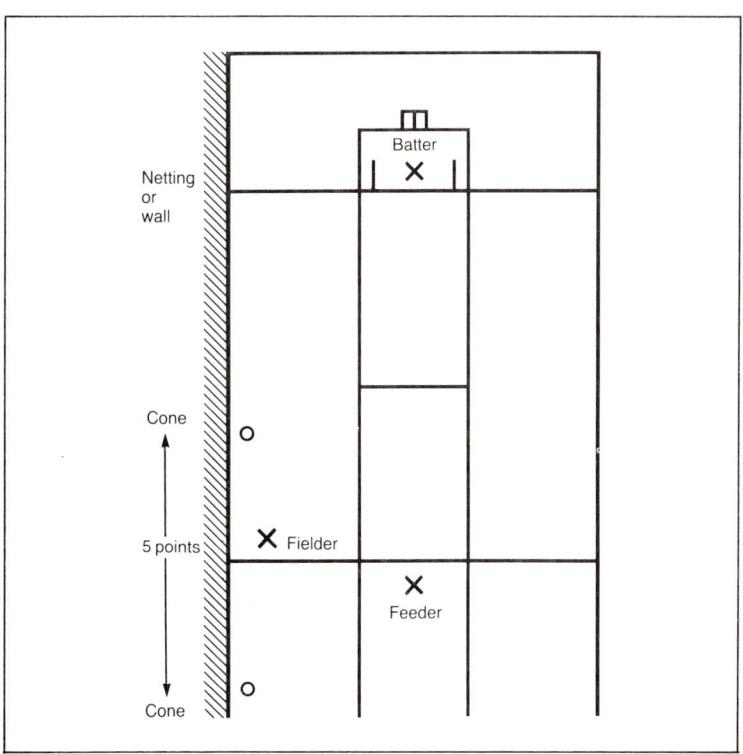

Batting practice – beating a fielder.

Batting practice – weight of shot.

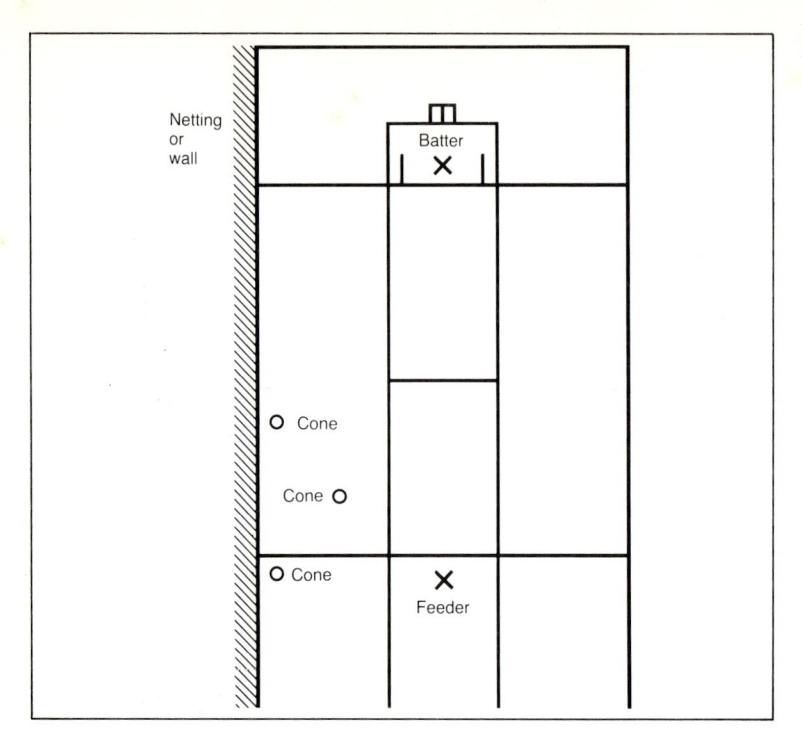

smaller. The cones can be placed anywhere on the court and in fact their position should vary. To make this competitive, everyone should have a turn with a scoring system of five points each time the ball settles within the triangle.

The block and run
This practice can be done in pairs providing that each pair has a wicket or target, possibly a cone. The feeder feeds the ball by tossing it in the air. The batter has to block the ball and run to the line where the feeder is standing and back to the batting crease. The feeder has to field the ball and attempt to run out the batter by hitting the target before the batter returns to the batting crease. Each of the pair has a turn, with a scoring system of five points for a run-out and two points each time the batter gets home safely.

BOWLING PRACTICES

The aim for most bowlers will be to put the ball intentionally on a particular length and line and to have control of this; in essence to be able to bowl accurately. This can only be achieved by regular practice at bowling at a target.

Target practice is intensive use of the bowling action so that a

Target practice for bowling.

93

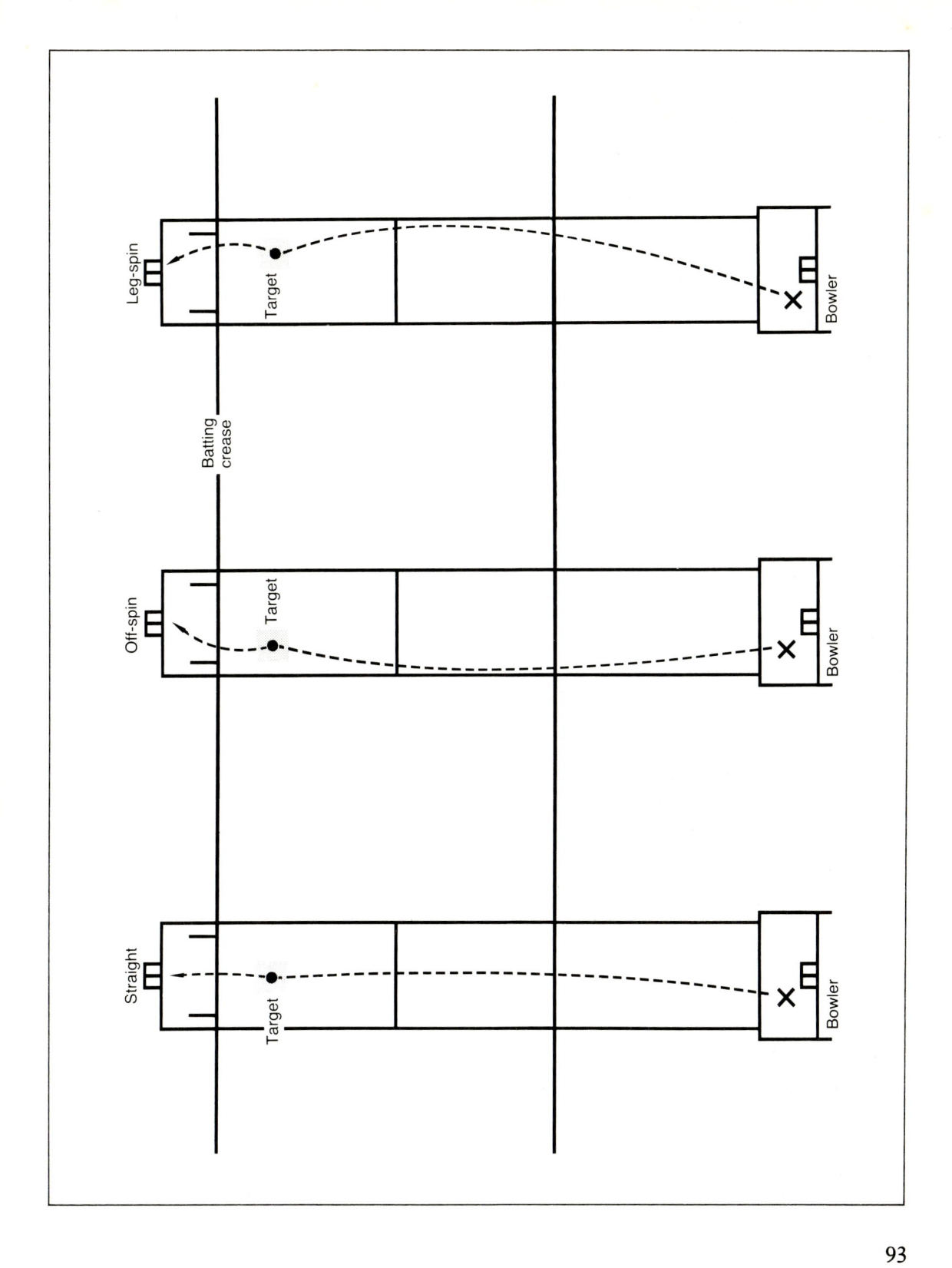

ball lands on the same area consistently. A target can be placed on the floor at whatever length and line the bowler wishes to practise and the aim is to pitch the ball on that target to score two points. It can be linked with accuracy on the stumps, so that if the bowler hits the target and the stumps he scores five points. This is useful not only for those bowling straight but also for spin-bowlers. The off-spin bowler could mark or place a target outside the off-stump and would need to spin the ball in from the target area to hit the stumps. Similarly, the leg-spin bowler can mark or place the target outside the leg-stump and would need to bring the ball back in to hit the stumps. Individuals can simply practise this alone, or an element of competition can be introduced by having two teams bowling at different targets and stumps for the same length of time. The teams total up their scores at the end of the period.

Underarm bowling
The rules for the underarm bowler are such that the novice often has problems making the ball pitch past the underarm line or releases the ball too late so that it hits the roof netting and therefore becomes a no-ball. A practice to help remedy this problem is simply to bowl the ball through a hoop.

One person stands a distance away from the bowler, holding a hoop at shoulder-height. This should be attempted first with the hoop five metres away from the bowler, the distance being increased up to fifteen metres as the bowler begins to get the ball through the hoop consistently.

All these practices can be developed further into game-like situations. In fact, the game of indoor cricket came about as a means of practising for traditional cricket. The more exciting and challenging practising can be made, the more teams will want to practise – and the more they practise, the better they will become at playing the fast and exciting game of indoor cricket.

Index

bats 13
batting 47–59
    angled 53
    backlift *48*
    block and run 57, 92
    checked off-drive 52
    cut 50
    grip *47*, *48*
    late cut 51
    leg-drive 54, *55*
    lofted drive 56
    order 75
    placement of ball 90
    practices 89, *91*, 92
    sliding *58*, *59*
    stance 47
    tactics 74
    weighting of ball 90
bowled 27
bowler, left-arm spin 41
    left-arm underarm 46
bowling 39–46
    grips for 37, 40–43, 45–46
    in-swing 41
    leg-spin 40
    length 46
    line 46
    off-spin 40
    order of 73
    out-swing 41
    overarm 37, *38*, *39*
    practices 92
    underarm 26, 43, 44, 45, 94

Cannon Ball Cricket (CBC) 11, 13, 18, 19, 20, 21, 24, 25, 32, 33, 34, 35, 36
captain 18
catching 77
    for wicketkeepers 88
    off the bat 79
    off the netting 78
caught 27
clothing 13
coaching, means of 9
competition 34
competitions, knock-out 36
concepts 10
court, floodlit 15
    layout 15, 17
    size 15
cricket, centre, first indoor 10
    continuous 9
    limited-over 9
    six-a-side 9

dismissals 27
Downton, Paul *12*

elbow-pads 13
equipment *13*, 21
eye-protectors 13

field-placings, attacking 71
    basic 18, 69, *70*
    defensive 72
fielding 60–64
    at back of court 62
    defensive 82
    diving for catch *64*
    for wicketkeepers 85
    ground, close to wicket 60, *61*
    hand and foot stops *63*
    practices 77
    tactics 69

games, conduct of 23
gloves 13, *47*, *48*
Gower, David *12*

Hanna, Paul 9
history 9
hit wicket 28

Indoor Cricket Arenas (ICA) 10, 18, 19, 20, 24, 33, 34, 35, 36
Indoor Cricket Federations 14
Indoor Cricket Stadiums (ICS) 11, 18, 19, 20, 21, 24, 25, 33, 34, 35, 36
innings, number per game 16
interference 29

Jones, Mick 9

knee-pads 13

lbw 28, *29*
leagues, graded 14, 34
Lloyd, Clive 14
Lord's Indoor Cricket School 9, 11, 22

'Mankad' 31, *32*

no-balls 24, 25, *26*

Packer, Kerry 9
penalties 35

rules 10, 15
    Cannon Ball (CBC) 18, 19, 20, 21, 24, 25, 32, 33, 34, 35, 36
    ICA 18, 19, 20, 21, 33, 34, 35, 36
    ICS 18, 19, 20, 21, 25, 33, 34, 35, 36

mixed 32
    Redball 19, 33, 34, 35
run out 30
running, between wickets 57
runs 16
    bonus 16

scoreboard, electronic 16, 22, 23
scoring 16, 21, 22
stumped 31
stumping 87
    leg-side 67
    off-side 66
substitutes 20, 34

tactics 69
    batting 74
    safety 73
techniques 37
training practices 77

umpire 16, 22, 23
underarm flick 80, *81*, *82*

wicketkeeper 20, 21
    catching 88
wicketkeeping 65
    practices 85
wides 24, 25